German
Traditional Cooking

This edition published in 1991
by Peter Ward Book Exports, Britannia House,
1 Parkway, London NW1 7PG, England
under licence from the proprietor.
Copyright ©: Kevin Weldon & Associates Pty Limited 1981
ISBN 1 86302 173 6.

Printed in Hong Kong by South China Printing Company
(1988) Limited

German
Traditional Cooking

Tony Schmaeling

PETER WARD

Acknowledgments

In November 1978, Kevin Weldon, at the time Managing Director of Paul Hamlyn and for many years a wining and dining companion, suggested that I write an international series of regional cookbooks. My thanks to Kevin – I blame him for everything.

Since then, I have had the pleasure of working with people like Warwick Jacobson, Anne Wilson and Helen Fraser, all members of the Hamlyn/Rigby staff, who gave me encouragement and technical support. Special thanks must go to my editor, Susan Tomnay, who was responsible for putting the whole thing together.

I thank my friend Warren Brash for his introduction to Graham Turnbull of Traveland, whose company made it possible for me to travel through Europe to collect material for this book. Graham's secretary Melinda Stevens was most helpful under adverse conditions, and kept the lines of communication open.

I also received great assistance from the Viva! Holidays' staff in London. My tour of Germany was organised with proverbial German efficiency and thoroughness by the German National Tourist Office. Their hospitality and generosity in providing hotel accommodation and arranging gastronomic and photographic appointments throughout the country made my journey comfortable, interesting and most enjoyable.

In Sydney, Manfred Staeuber at the German Tourist Office gave me valuable assistance before my departure and on my return to Sydney. In Frankfurt at the DZT, Uwe Woggon and Frau Ager, with professional efficiency, arranged an itinerary which took me to most parts of the country.

Uwe Woggon, who joined me on my travels, was a knowledgeable guide and entertaining travel companion.

My tour of Germany started with a visit to Wehlen on the Moselle River, where I had spent a happy eighteen months in my youth, and where a meal with my school friend Manfred Prüm and his wife, washed down with some Wehlener Sonnenuhr from his famous vineyard, brought back pleasant memories.

During my travels through Germany, the interest shown in the project, the hospitality, and the generous sharing of kitchen secrets all contributed to the success of the venture.

We'd like to thank Peter Lamb's Game Butchery in Mosman, Handler Butchers in Double Bay and Tom & Frank Greengrocers in Sydney for supplying facilities for photography.

Contents

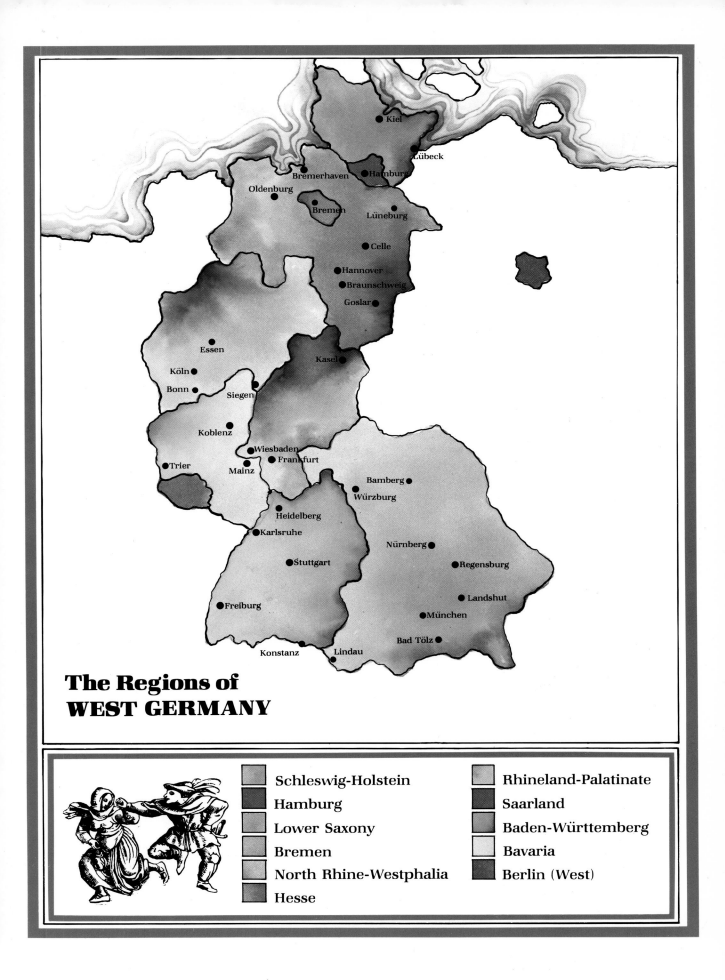

The Regions of
WEST GERMANY

Kiel
Lübeck
Bremerhaven
Hamburg
Oldenburg
Bremen
Lüneburg
Celle
Hannover
Braunschweig
Goslar
Essen
Kasel
Köln
Bonn
Siegen
Koblenz
Wiesbaden
Trier
Frankfurt
Mainz
Bamberg
Würzburg
Heidelberg
Karlsruhe
Nürnberg
Stuttgart
Regensburg
Landshut
Freiburg
München
Bad Tölz
Konstanz
Lindau

Schleswig-Holstein

Hamburg

Lower Saxony

Bremen

North Rhine-Westphalia

Hesse

Rhineland-Palatinate

Saarland

Baden-Württemberg

Bavaria

Berlin (West)

Introduction

Ask anyone not familiar with German cooking to name some typical German dishes, and the replies will be very similar: potatoes, hearty soups, beer, sausages (Wurst), Sauerkraut, Speck, pork, herrings.

While this list does not give the full picture, these foods certainly do form a vital part of German cooking.

The regional patterns and specialities are no longer clearly defined as they were some hundred years ago, before Bismarck unified the German-speaking kingdoms, dukedoms and other states under the Imperial crown. In those days, the regional differences between the various sovereign areas were easy to identify. You knew when you were in Bavaria or Saxony, Württemberg or Schleswig-Holstein, by the type of food you were offered.

Today, after several wars and a great deal of social unheaval and population movement, the formal regional divisions no longer exist.

While in many respects Germans are conservative and content with traditional ways when it comes to food, they have always been willing to adopt innovations and absorb external influences. There is no better example of this than the post-war influence on German cooking of American fast foods. Ease of movement and travel have given all sections of the German population a better view of foreign cooking, and experiencing the dishes of other countries has influenced their own approach to food.

So, what has happened to the traditional cooking of Germany? Fortunately it still exists, although it is no longer dominant.

It is difficult to imagine a German table without its Kartoffeln (potatoes) in one form or another. In the Rhineland they will appear as Himmel und Erde (Heaven and Earth) cooked with apples and Blutwurst (a type of black pudding), thus combining the two most characteristic of German ingredients, potatoes and sausage. Bavaria's potato salad, and its Kartoffel Knödel (potato dumplings) are common in most parts of the country.

Hearty soups are the staple diet of cold climates, so it is not surprising that in the north of Germany one finds more soups than in the south. Fish soups are among their specialities. However, Germans love soups in general, and Mittagessen (the main midday meal) almost always includes a plate of warming soup.

Volumes could be written about German sausages, and the Wurst has a special place in every German's heart. The names of many give away their origins: Braunschweiger Leberwurst, Stuttgarter Presskopf, Thüringer Blutwurst, Hamburger Mettwurst, Holsteiner Kochwurst and many others.

It is not really surprising that Wurst is so popular in Germany. Germans are very fond of pork, and pigs are bred extensively in all parts of the country. Speck, the smoked bacon, is another by-product which is closely associated with German cooking. Among the best in the land is Westphalian Speck which, with Westphalian ham, finds its way to most German tables. Speck is used extensively and gives many of the country's dishes their characteristic smoky scent and flavour.

Sauerkraut, known since prehistoric times, has found its modern home in Germany. Whether cooked, raw, in salads, or as part of a made-up dish, it is eaten throughout the country.

The German Konditorei, or cake shop, is an institution shared only with Austria. The Germans like their Kuchen mit Kaffee, and the pastry repertoire is extensive. If the Kuchen lack the lightness of their French cousins or the frivolity of their Austrian relations, it is only because the Germans like them more solid.

The herring is another German institution. Despite its northern origin, it is popular in all parts of the land, although it probably tastes best along the shores of the North or Baltic Seas.

There are many other characteristic German dishes which form part of a foreigner's concept of German cooking, and a great number of these are associated with specific parts of the country. I have tried to present some of the traditional German dishes, most of them collected during my trip through the country, and hope that they will inspire the traveller through Germany to seek out and enjoy the local dishes. Guten Appetit!

First Courses (Vorspeisen)

It is the purpose of the first course to awaken, stimulate and excite the appetite in preparation for the meal to follow.

In Germany, eating habits and traditions have changed over the last 70 years, but especially since the Second World War. Today the number of courses served, as well as the quantities eaten have become smaller.

Soup is still a popular way of starting a meal, especially the Mittagessen, the main mid-day meal. However, more and more frequently, a piquant, sharp and appetising first course dish is finding its way to the German table.

Appropriately, they call them the Vorspeisen, the 'before dining', and their range and variety is very wide. Simple canapés with pâté, smoked salmon or herrings are passed around before the guests are called to the table. An immense number of ingenious salads with creamy mayonnaises, sour cream, fish, herrings, meats, sausages and cooked vegetables in tasty, tangy and colourful combinations, appear on the table. Most of them can be bought in the great German institution — the delicatessen shops — or are lovingly prepared at home.

Eggs in piquant sauces tempt the palate while the glowing pink of the Roterübensalat (Beetroot salad) with cubes of meat, sausage or herrings not only taste great but also delight the eye.

Sweet and sour dishes are eaten frequently as many Germans have a strongly developed palate for pickled, sour and vinegary food. So it is not surprising to see dishes like pickled herrings, rollmops and various herring salads.

Most Vorspeisen are served cold, frequently in aspic, like Aal in Gelee (Jellied eel) and the different types of Sülze or brawns. However, there is also the ever-popular Bratwurst and Blutwurst which are often served warm.

Vineyard snails, now quite rare, are sometimes prepared in a pastry crust and served with herb butter.

German cooks are inventive and the already large repertoire of Vorspeisen is constantly being enriched with new and tasty additions.

Three typical German first course dishes: Cabbage Rolls, Stuffed Mushrooms and Herring Salad.

Gurkensalat
Cucumber Salad

Serves 4

1 large cucumber
½ teaspoon salt
1 tablespoon sugar

1 tablespoon white wine vinegar
¼ cup (2 fl oz) sour cream
1 tablespoon chopped parsley

1. Peel the cucumber leaving some of the green rind. Slice it very thinly. The cucumber may be served either fresh or marinated. When serving it fresh, sprinkle the cucumber with salt, sugar and vinegar, mix in the sour cream and sprinkle with the parsley.
2. Alternatively, mix the salt and sugar into the vinegar, and marinate the cucumber in this mixture for 30 minutes. Drain off the liquid, mix the sour cream with the cucumber, and serve sprinkled with parsley.

Allgäuer Käsesalat
Cheese Salad

Serves 4-6

2 cups (11 oz) diced Swiss-type cheese
¼ cup (1 oz) chopped onions
1 dill cucumber, peeled and thinly sliced
1 cup diced fresh fruit in season
4 tablespoons oil

2 tablespoons white wine vinegar
2 tablespoons water
1 tablespoon sugar
salt
freshly ground black pepper

1. Combine all ingredients and marinate for 20 minutes. Serve on lettuce leaves.

Bayerischer Kartoffelsalat
Bavarian Potato Salad

This recipe comes from the Goldene Sonne in Landshut.
Landshut is one of the many picturesque Bavarian towns whose sixteenth and seventeenth century character has been carefully and sensitively preserved.
The Goldene Sonne stands on the Neustadt, a wide street which is almost a long rectangular market-place surrounded by beautifully maintained houses and gaily painted buildings.
It has been an inn since 1550 and has been owned by the family of the present landlord for over fifty years.
Mine host is a huge, friendly Bavarian whose rosy cheeks bear witness to many a Stein of the excellent Hackenbräu beer which he serves.
The food is traditionally Bavarian too: suckling piglet; Weiss and Bratwurst (famous Bavarian sausages from his own butcher shop); succulent veal knuckles; and of course, the inevitable potato salad and bread roll dumplings.

Serves 6-8

750 g-1 kg (1½-2 lb) new potatoes
2 onions, finely chopped
DRESSING
½ cup (4 fl oz) oil
3 tablespoons lemon juice
salt
freshly ground black pepper
½ teaspoon sugar

OPTIONAL ADDITIONS OF WHICH ONE OR SEVERAL MAY BE USED:
1 tablespoon borage, basil, tarragon, parsley, chives
1-2 apples, peeled and finely chopped
1-2 pickled cucumbers, finely chopped

1. Boil the potatoes, making sure that they are not too soft. Cool them and peel.
2. Cut them into slices and place them in a mixing bowl with the chopped onions.
3. Prepare the dressing by vigorously mixing all the ingredients together.
4. While the potatoes are still warm, pour the dressing over them and mix them gently. Serve at room temperature.

Roterüben Salat
Beetroot and Endive Salad

This dish has a tasty combination of flavours. If endive is not available, firm hearts of lettuce, broken up into small pieces, may be used.

Serves 4

2 medium-sized beetroot, cooked and
  diced
3 endives, sliced
1 cooking apple, peeled, cored and
  finely diced
1 small onion, finely chopped
2 tablespoons prepared horse-radish
2 egg yolks

juice of 1 lemon
3 tablespoons sour cream
½ teaspoon mustard
1 teaspoon sugar (optional)
salt
freshly ground black pepper
3 tablespoons oil
chopped parsley for garnish

1. In a bowl mix beetroot, endives, apple, onion and horse-radish.
2. In a mixing bowl, combine egg yolks, lemon juice, sour cream, mustard, sugar, salt and pepper.
3. Mix for 5 minutes and then, still mixing, gradually add the oil.
4. Pour the dressing over the salad and serve garnished with parsley.

Pfifferlingsalat auf Bremer Art
Pickled Mushrooms

A mixture of two or more types of mushrooms adds variety to this piquant starter.

Serves 4

375 g (12 oz) pfifferlings or small, firm,
  button mushrooms
½ small onion, finely chopped
1 capsicum (pepper), seeded and
  chopped
1 stalk celery, finely chopped
1 tablespoon capers

2 sprigs parsley, finely chopped
3 tablespoons white wine or cider
  vinegar
2 tablespoons olive oil
salt
freshly ground black pepper

1. Place the mushrooms in a glass or china dish.
2. Combine and mix the remaining ingredients and pour them over the mushrooms.
3. Refrigerate for 24 hours and serve on crisp lettuce leaves.

Sauerkraut Salat
Sauerkraut Salad

Serves 4

500 g (1 lb) Sauerkraut
2 apples peeled, cored and diced
½ cup bottled mixed pickles, diced
1 onion, finely chopped
2 tablespoons chopped dill

2 tablespoons chopped parsley
salt
freshly ground black pepper
2 tablespoons sugar
2 slices bacon, diced

1. In a salad bowl, combine all the ingredients except the bacon. Taste before adding salt as the Sauerkraut may be sufficiently salty.
2. Fry the bacon until crisp and then add it and its melted fat to the salad as a dressing.
3. Chill and serve cold.

Sauerkrautkuchen
Sauerkraut Pie

Serves 6

PASTRY
2 cups (8 oz) self-raising flour
½ teaspoon salt
185 g (6 oz) butter
1 egg, beaten
1 tablespoon cream (optional)
1 egg white, unbeaten

FILLING
125 g (4 oz) bacon, diced
4 frankfurters, sliced
1 onion, chopped
750 g (1½ lb) Sauerkraut, well drained
1 cup (8 fl oz) cream
¼ cup (2 fl oz) tomato purée
1 teaspoon paprika
salt

Pastry
1. Preheat the oven to 190°C (375°F/Gas 5).
2. Combine the flour and the salt. Dice the butter and work it into the flour until it is the consistency of breadcrumbs. Add the egg and mix until pliable. Add the cream if the dough is not sufficiently moist.
3. Roll out the dough and press it into the bottom and sides of a round pie dish 23 cm (9 in) in diameter. Brush the bottom with the egg white.
4. Reserve the dough trimmings for a lattice topping.

Filling
1. Sauté the bacon and the frankfurters until light brown. Add the onion and continue to sauté until soft. Add the Sauerkraut and simmer for 20 minutes.
2. Place the mixture in the pastry flan.
3. Combine the cream, tomato purée, paprika and salt. Mix well and pour over the Sauerkraut.
4. Roll out the remaining dough, cut it into strips and place them in a lattice pattern on top of the pie.
5. Bake for 40 to 50 minutes until the crust is golden.

Mayschoss an der Ahr

Germany is best known for its white wines and one does not associate it with reds. However the town of Mayschoss has the oldest vintners' associations in Germany and along the slopes of the Ahr valley is the largest red wine growing area in the country. It's a quiet countryside. There is good game hunting in the surrounding Eifel mountains and numerous mineral springs supply many of the mineral waters available in Germany.

The nearby Nürburg Ring is one of the best-known car racing circuits in the land.

Rettichsalat
Radish Salad

Serves 4

2 bunches radishes, thinly sliced
½ cup (4 fl oz) sour cream
2 tablespoons wine vinegar
½ teaspoon sugar
salt

freshly ground black pepper
100 g (3½ oz) cream or cottage cheese,
  crumbed
2 tablespoons finely chopped chives

1. In a bowl combine radishes, sour cream, vinegar, sugar, salt and pepper and mix gently together.
2. Transfer to a shallow serving dish. Sprinkle with the cheese and serve garnished with chives.

Überbackener Spinat mit Käse
Baked Spinach and Cheese

Serves 4

750 g (1½ lb) fresh spinach leaves
100 g (3½ oz) butter
1 onion, finely chopped
1 clove garlic, crushed
salt

freshly ground black pepper
¼ teaspoon nutmeg
1 teaspoon paprika
125 g (4 oz) grated Gruyère-type cheese

1. Preheat the oven to 180°C (350°F/Gas 4).
2. In a large saucepan boil some water. Plunge the spinach into it and boil for 5 minutes.
3. Drain, dry, and coarsely chop the spinach.
4. In a saucepan melt the butter. Fry the onion and garlic until the onion is soft and transparent.
5. Add the spinach and sauté lightly until most of the moisture has evaporated.
6. Season and add nutmeg and paprika.
7. Grease an oven-proof dish. Sprinkle the bottom and sides with half of the cheese. Place the spinach in the dish, level the top and sprinkle with the rest of the cheese.
8. Bake for 20 to 30 minutes until the cheese melts. Serve hot.

Maultaschen
Swabian Ravioli

Serves 4

1 recipe Spätzle dough (see p. 140)
FILLING
375 g (12 oz) pork, minced
1 tablespoon butter
1 onion, finely chopped
500 g (1 lb) fresh raw spinach, cooked
  and chopped

2 slices stale white bread, soaked in
  water
1 egg
1 teaspoon salt
freshly ground black pepper
¼ teaspoon nutmeg

1. In a saucepan, sauté the pork in butter. Add the onion and spinach.
2. Squeeze the water out of the bread, and add the bread to the pork/spinach mixture. Mix in the egg, salt, pepper and nutmeg.
3. Roll out the Spätzle dough and cut it into small squares. Place a teaspoon of the filling on each square. Fold over and seal the edge. These are the Maultaschen.
4. Boil some salted water in a saucepan and drop the Maultaschen, 6 at a time, into the water. Cook for 10 minutes until they rise to the surface. Remove with a slotted spoon and drain. The Maultaschen can be served either with melted butter or a sauce of your choice. They are also delicious when cooked in a consommé.

Zwiebelkuchen
Onion Pie

Serves 8

PASTRY
2 cups (8 oz) self-raising flour
½ teaspoon salt
185 g (6 oz) butter
1 egg, beaten
1 tablespoon cream (optional)
1 egg white, lightly beaten

FILLING
250 g (8 oz) onions, chopped
2 slices bacon, diced
2 tablespoons butter
¼ teaspoon salt
1 teaspoon caraway seeds
½ tablespoon flour
½ cup (4 fl oz) cream
2 eggs, beaten

Pastry
1. Preheat the oven to 190°C (375°F/Gas 5).
2. Combine the flour and salt. Dice the butter and rub into the flour until the mixture is the consistency of breadcrumbs. Add the egg and blend until the dough is pliable. Add the cream if the dough is not sufficiently moist.
3. Roll out the dough and press it into the bottom and sides of a round pie dish 23 cm (9 in) in diameter. Brush the egg white over the bottom of the dough.

Filling
1. Sauté the onions and bacon in the butter until soft, then add the salt and caraway seeds. Stir in the flour and slowly add the cream.
2. Remove from the heat, add the beaten eggs and mix well together. Pour into the pastry-lined pie dish.
3. Bake until the pastry is golden and the filling is firm. Serve as a snack with white wine.

Fischsalat
Fish Salad

Serves 4

4 fish fillets
30 g (1 oz) butter
juice of 1 lemon
½ cup (4 fl oz) water or dry white wine
2 tablespoons sour cream
1 tablespoon mustard

½ small onion, thinly sliced
salt
freshly ground black pepper
4 lemon slices
3 sprigs parsley, finely chopped

1. Lightly poach the fish fillets in the butter, lemon juice, water or wine for 5 minutes.
2. Carefully remove the fish, place them in a serving dish and when cold cut the fillets into 2.5 cm (1 in) pieces.
3. Cool the cooking juice, add sour cream, mustard, onion, salt and pepper, mix well and pour it over the fish.
4. Refrigerate and serve cold garnished with lemon slices and parsley.

Krabben in Leichter Sosse
Prawns with Yoghurt Dressing

From the Park Hotel Fürstenhof in Celle.

Serves 4

345 g (11 oz) cooked prawns (shrimps),
   peeled
1 cup (8 fl oz) light yoghurt
1 tablespoon mayonnaise (see p. 138)
1 tablespoon tomato sauce
salt

freshly ground black pepper
1 teaspoon horse-radish relish
½ teaspoon sugar
1 tablespoon brandy

1. Divide the prawns into 4 portions.
2. To make the sauce, combined all the remaining ingredients.
3. Arrange the prawns on individual plates and serve the sauce separately in a sauce boat.

Lachstüten mit Meerrettich Rahm
Salmon with Horse-radish Cream

In Germany, horse-radish cream is a popular garnish for smoked salmon. This is one of the many ways it can be served.

Serves 4

1 cup (8 fl oz) cream, whipped
1 tablespoon horse-radish relish
1 tablespoon vinegar or juice of 1
   lemon
½ teaspoon sugar
salt

freshly ground black pepper
1 teaspoon gelatine, dissolved in ¼ cup
   (2 fl oz) hot water, cooled
12 slices smoked salmon
2 sprigs parsley, finely chopped

1. Combine all ingredients except the smoked salmon and parsley.
2. Form the salmon slices into cones and with a teaspoon or piping bag fill the cones with the cream.
3. Arrange the cones on a serving platter and refrigerate for 2 hours or until cream hardens.
4. Serve chilled, the cream sprinkled with parsley.

Hummersalat mit Gurken
Crayfish Salad with Cucumber

Serves 4

flesh of 1 crayfish, diced, or 8
   medium-sized king prawns (shrimps),
   shelled, de-veined and sliced
2 large cucumbers, peeled, seeded and
   diced
½ cup (4 fl oz) mayonnaise (see p. 138)
1 tablespoon tomato paste
1 teaspoon dry mustard
2 tablespoons prepared mustard

2 tablespoons dry sherry
1 tablespoon brandy
juice of ½ lemon
½ small onion, finely chopped
3 sprigs dill, finely chopped
2 sprigs tarragon, finely chopped or
   1 teaspoon dried tarragon
salt
freshly ground black pepper

1. Place the crayfish or prawns in a serving dish.
2. In a bowl combine all the remaining ingredients. Mix well and pour them over the crayfish or prawns. Toss gently.
3. Refrigerate for 2 to 3 hours and serve cold or at room temperature.

Opposite: Breakfast at the Gastof Schütte.
Clockwise from bottom left: German breads; Ham on the Bone;
Liver Sausage; Black Pudding.

Gasthof Schütte, Schmallenberg-Oberkirchen

The hotel and restaurant Schütte is situated in a romantic village surrounded by the rolling hills of the Sauerland in Westphalia.

The restaurant specialises in sausages and hams, especially Westphalian ham. The menu also offers venison, boar and other game dishes, which come from the forest surrounding the local township.

Germans enjoy breakfast, and at the Schütte one can start the day with sausages, smoked hams, a selection of cheeses, eggs, and many varieties of local bread, including the famous black Pumpernickel which originated in Westphalia.

Gasthof Schütte prides itself on its preparation of saddle of venison, which is served with fresh mushrooms from the local forests. The ham served at the Schütte comes from their own smoke-room.

Krebssalat Helgoländer Art
Helgoland Crayfish, Rice and Mayonnaise Salad

Serves 4

315 g (10 oz) cooked crayfish or
   prawns (shrimps), cut into chunks
1 cup (5 oz) cooked rice
2 tablespoons curry powder
¾ cup (6 fl oz) mayonnaise (see p. 138)
¼ cup (2 fl oz) sour cream

2 eggs, hard boiled and chopped
juice ½ lemon
¼ teaspoon salt
freshly ground black pepper
1 tablespoon chopped dill or chives

1. Combine the crayfish or prawns with the cooked rice.
2. Mix the curry powder, mayonnaise and sour cream together and blend into the prawns and rice.
3. Add the eggs, lemon juice, salt, pepper and dill or chives. Serve on lettuce leaves.

Hering in Saurer Sahne
Herrings in Sour Cream

A very popular first course in north Germany.

Serves 4

6 Matjes herring fillets
1 cup (8 fl oz) sour cream
juice 1 lemon or 2 tablespoons white
   wine vinegar
½ tablespoon sugar (optional)

freshly ground black pepper
1 apple, peeled, cored and cut into thin
   slivers
1 onion, cut into thin slices
1 tablespoon finely chopped dill

1. Cut the herring fillets into 2.5 cm (1 in) pieces and arrange them on a serving dish.
2. Mix the sour cream, lemon juice or vinegar and (if desired) the sugar. Add the pepper and let the mixture stand for 10 minutes.
3. Arrange the apple slivers and onion slices in a layer on the herrings.
4. Cover with the cream and sprinkle with dill.

Heringssalat Rheinischer Art
Rhineland Herring, Apple and Vegetable Salad

Serves 6

6 pickled herring fillets, chopped
155 g (5 oz) beetroot, cooked and diced
1 large apple, cored and diced
2 medium potatoes, cooked and diced
1 small onion, finely chopped
½ cup (2 oz) chopped walnuts
½ cup (4 fl oz) sour cream

½ cup (4 fl oz) mayonnaise (see p. 138)
1 teaspoon sugar
1 egg, hard-boiled and sliced for
   garnish
6-8 slices beetroot for garnish
1 tablespoon finely chopped parsley
   or dill

1. Combine all the ingredients except the egg, sliced beetroot, and parsley or dill. Mix the ingredients gently together and arrange them in a salad bowl or on a serving platter.
2. Decorate the top with the egg slices and the beetroot. Before serving, sprinkle with the parsley or dill.

Hamburger Heringssalat

Herring and Apple Salad

From Donners Hotel in Cuxhaven.
The restaurant at the Donners Hotel is well known for its Matjes herring smorgasbords. Unfortunately, I missed this feast, but the impressive variety of herring dishes was described to me: Matjes with horse-radish, sour cream sauce, onion rings, cucumber, orange slices and pineapple; Matjes served with a sauce containing onions, cucumbers, champignons, cream, yoghurt, ketchup, and raw egg yolk, served with several varieties of bread; several Matjes salads; Matjes 'pots'; Matjes rolls; an almost endless variety of combinations.
Cuxhaven may be an uninspiring harbour town, but the Donners is a mecca for those who love Matjes herrings.

Serves 4

½ cup (4 fl oz) sour cream
1 tablespoon vinegar or juice of
  1 lemon
freshly ground black pepper
1 teaspoon prepared horse-radish
4 Matjes herring fillets, cut into 2.5 cm
  (1 in) pieces

2 small onions, thinly sliced
1 firm apple, peeled, quartered, cored
  and thinly sliced
lettuce leaves
1 egg, hard-boiled and sliced
1 green or red capsicum (pepper),
  halved, seeded and cut into strips

1. In a bowl combine sour cream, vinegar or lemon juice, pepper and horse-radish.
2. To this dressing add herrings, onions and apple, and mix gently together.
3. Refrigerate for 2 to 3 hours.
4. To serve, divide salad into 4 portions, heap onto 4 lettuce leaves, and garnish with slices of hard-boiled egg and capsicum strips.

Eier in Grüner Sosse

Eggs in Green Sauce

A speciality of Frankfurt.

Serves 4

½ cup (4 fl oz) sour cream
½ cup (4 fl oz) yogurt
½ cup (4 fl oz) mayonnaise (see p. 138)
3 sprigs each of the following fresh
  herbs (or any combination): dill,
  parsley, tarragon, oregano
1 small bunch chives

juice of 1 lemon
1 egg, hard-boiled and finely chopped
salt
freshly ground black pepper
½ teaspoon sugar (optional)
8 eggs, hard-boiled and cut in half
finely chopped dill for garnish

1. Combine sour cream, yogurt and mayonnaise.
2. Finely chop the herbs by hand or in a food processor.
3. Mix the sauce, chopped herbs, lemon juice, chopped egg, salt, pepper and (if desired) sugar.
4. Arrange the egg halves on a serving platter, pour the sauce over them and serve chilled, garnished with chopped dill.

Hirn Überbacken

Brains au Gratin

Serves 4

4 veal brains (or 6 lambs' brains)
2 tablespoons vinegar
1 teaspoon salt
45 g (1½ oz) butter
45 g (1½ oz) flour
⅔ cup (5½ fl oz) hot beef stock
  (see p. 136)
⅔ cup (5½ fl oz) hot milk
45 g (1½ oz) grated Parmesan cheese
½ teaspoon Worcestershire sauce
1 egg yolk
3 tablespoons cream
freshly ground black pepper
dry breadcrumbs

TOPPING
¼ cup (1 oz) grated Parmesan cheese
30 g (1 oz) butter, cut into small pieces

1. Preheat the oven to 200°C (400°F/Gas 6).
2. Remove the membranes from the brains.
3. Half fill a saucepan with water, add the vinegar and salt, plunge the brains into it and simmer for 5 minutes. Remove them with a slotted spoon and rinse them under running cold water.
4. Chop the brains into cubes.
5. To make the sauce, melt the butter, add the flour and cook for 5 minutes.
6. Add the hot stock and milk or, if you have no stock, use all milk.
7. Cook, stirring constantly until the sauce is thick and smooth.
8. Remove from the heat, stir in the cheese, Worcestershire sauce, egg yolk, cream, pepper and salt.
9. Add the brains and pour the mixture into a buttered soufflé dish sprinkled with breadcrumbs.
10. Sprinkle the top with the cheese and dot with pieces of butter.
11. Place it in the preheated oven and cook for 10-15 minutes or until the top browns.
12. Serve it with toast as a first course.

Celle

The town of Celle is one of the best preserved examples of the half timbered style of architecture.

Undamaged during the Second World War, some of the houses date back to the 16th Century.

A stroll along the many pedestrian streets among the colourful buildings conjures up images of past ages. The castle, originally the residence of the Duke of Brunswick and Lüneburg, became one of the palaces of the Electors and Kings of Hanover. The theatre in the castle, built in 1670 is Germany's oldest existing theatre.

Historically the town is linked with the crown of England. The principality of Lüneburg was united with the Electorate of Hanover and Princess Dorothea, the daughter of the last duke married George Ludwig of Hanover who later became George I of England.

Celle, situated at the edge of the Lüneburg Heath is the starting point for excursions into the peaceful beauty of the National Park of the southern heath.

Geräucherter Zungensalat
Smoked Ox-tongue Salad

Serves 4-6

1 smoked ox-tongue
1 garlic clove, peeled
3 cloves
6 peppercorns
3 bay leaves
½ cup (4 fl oz) olive oil

3 tablespoons wine or cider vinegar, or juice of 1 lemon
½ small onion, finely sliced
freshly ground black pepper
4-6 lettuce leaves
3 sprigs parsley, finely chopped

1. In a large saucepan simmer the tongue together with the garlic, cloves, peppercorns and bay leaves for 2½ to 3 hours or until tender.
2. Allow to cool in the water.
3. When cool enough to handle, skin the tongue and remove gristle and fat. Slice it, and cut each slice into fine julienne strips.
4. Place the strips into a serving dish.
5. In a screw top jar mix and shake the oil and vinegar or lemon juice.
6. Add the onion and pepper to the dressing. Taste the tongue for saltiness before using any salt. (Most smoked tongue is well salted.)
7. Pour the dressing over the tongue and toss well. Refrigerate and toss again, and serve at room temperature on lettuce leaves. Garnish with parsley.

Gänseleber Pâté
Goose Liver Pâté

Serves 6

375 g (12 oz) goose, duck or chicken livers
125 g (4 oz) butter
2 sprigs thyme, chopped
½ teaspoon powdered bay leaves
2 sprigs rosemary, chopped

½ cup (4 fl oz) dry sherry
1 tablespoon brandy
1 teaspoon honey
salt
freshly ground black pepper

1. Lightly sauté the livers in the butter so that they are still pink inside.
2. Add herbs, sherry, brandy, honey, salt and pepper and simmer for 2 minutes.
3. Finely purée the mixture, one cupful at a time, in a food processor or blender.
4. Pack into an earthenware jar and refrigerate for 24 hours.
5. Serve cold on small pieces of toasted rye bread.

Fleischsalat auf Bremer Art
Bremen Meat Salad with Frankfurters and Mayonnaise

Serves 6

125g (4 oz) boiled ham, cut into thin strips
2 frankfurters, diced
60g (2 oz) salami, diced
3 gherkins, diced

¼ cup (2 fl oz) mayonnaise (see p. 138)
1 tablespoon white wine vinegar
salt
freshly ground black pepper

1. Combine all ingredients and mix them gently together. Serve on lettuce leaves.

Leber Süss-Saur
Sweet and Sour Calf's Liver

Serves 4

100 g (3½ oz) Speck or smoked bacon,
  diced
1 onion, roughly chopped
375 g (12 oz) calf's liver, thinly sliced
2 tablespoons flour
½ cup (4 fl oz) dry white wine

½ cup (4 fl oz) sour cream
1 tablespoon sugar
2 tablespoons wine vinegar
salt
freshly ground black pepper

1. Over medium heat, fry the Speck or bacon.
2. Add the onion and sauté until soft and transparent.
3. Dust the liver slices with flour and sauté them lightly for 2-3 minutes.
4. Add the rest of the ingredients and simmer for 5 minutes. Adjust amount of sugar and vinegar to suit your taste.

Bauernfrühstück
Farmer's Breakfast with Eggs and Bacon

Serves 4

6 slices bacon
1 tablespoon butter
1 onion, chopped
4 potatoes, cooked and finely diced

6 eggs
½ teaspoon salt
freshly ground black pepper
¼ cup (2 fl oz) milk

1. In a frying pan, fry the bacon until it is crisp. Remove and drain on absorbent paper. When cool, chop into small pieces.
2. Pour off the bacon fat from the frying pan, add the butter and sauté the onion until soft. Add the potatoes and brown lightly.
3. Beat the eggs lightly and add the salt, pepper and milk, and finally the chopped bacon.
4. Pour the egg mixture over the onions and potatoes and turn with an egg slice until cooked.
5. Serve with buttered Pumpernickel and cucumber salad (see p. 12).

Soups

There are probably no other people who love soup as much as the Germans. While Vorspeisen (first courses) play an important part in a German menu, it is hard to imagine a Mittagsessen, the main meal of the day, without the soup. The Germans not only have an appropriate soup for special occasions, but every season has its soups. In addition to this there are regional soups and it was once possible to tell the diner's social standing by the type of soup he was eating.

In today's Germany, most vegetables and other ingredients are available the whole year round; special occasions are not as strictly and traditionally observed and upheavals during the past few generations have erased most class distinctions once so strong in this nation, while modern transport and communications have helped in the exchange of regional culinary secrets.

Nevertheless, in spring, when the first fresh local vegetables appear on the stalls, Germans like to prepare Klare Gemüsesuppe (Clear Vegetable Soup) or velvety Spargelcremesuppe, the popular Asparagus Cream Soup. When it is hot in summer, there is nothing more pleasant than a cold Apple Soup or a refreshing Weinsuppe, made with a crisp German white wine.

However, the Germans excel in their hearty, stick-to-the-ribs winter soups. When the snow is on the ground and an icy wind blows outside what could be better to lift the frozen spirit than a Kartoffelsuppe, the most typical of German soup, with its chunks of frankfurter sausages or smoky pork.

From the shores of the North and Baltic Seas come the many fish soups and chowders which are now so popular throughout the country.

Today as in the past it is difficult to imagine an elegant dinner party without the very refined yet aromatic Kraftbrühe, a clear consommé which satisfies the initial appetite but does not detract from the dishes to follow.

At the other end of the scale are the various heavy and nourishing Bauernsuppen, the farmer's soups, the beer and bread soups, those made with Sauerkraut and solid dumplings, many of them eaten as a whole meal and then washed down with steins of local beer.

Liver Dumpling Soup (see p. 30)

Kartoffelsuppe
Potato Soup

No set of German soup recipes would be complete without potato soup which is a national favourite.

Serves 6

4 cups (litre) chicken stock
  (see p. 134)
2 cups (12 oz) finely diced potatoes
2 spring onions (scallions), chopped

2 cups (16 fl oz) milk
1 teaspoon Worcestershire sauce
½ cup (4 fl oz) sour cream

1. Cook the potatoes and spring onions in the chicken stock until the potatoes are soft (15 to 20 minutes).
2. In a food processor or blender, purée the potatoes, onions and chicken stock and return them to the saucepan.
3. Add the milk and Worcestershire sauce and heat through. Before serving, season and add the sour cream. The soup may be served hot or chilled.

Kartoffelsuppe auf Schwäbische Art
Swabian Potato Soup

Serves 8

3 potatoes, peeled and thinly sliced
1 small onion, chopped
2 tablespoons butter
2 cups (10 oz) diced cooked meat (beef or veal)

8 cups (2 litres) water or beef stock
  (see p. 136)
salt
freshly ground black pepper
2 cups cooked Spätzle (see p. 140)

1. Sauté the potatoes and onions in the butter until they are golden brown. Add the meat and the water or stock, and season.
2. Simmer until the potatoes are very soft, then add the Spätzle, heat for 2-3 minutes and serve hot.

Badische Lauchsuppe
Baden Leek Soup

Serves 4

3 leeks, white part only
90 g (3 oz) butter
1 large onion, chopped
4 cups (1 litre) chicken stock
  (see p. 134)

salt
freshly ground black pepper
1 cup (8 fl oz) milk
¾ cup (4 oz) ham, cut into julienne
  strips

1. Wash the leeks thoroughly and slice them into 2.5 cm (1 in) pieces.
2. In a heavy-bottomed saucepan, melt the butter and sauté the leeks and onions until they are soft.
3. Add the chicken stock, salt and pepper and simmer for 10 minutes, stirring occasionally.
4. Add the milk and bring gently to the boil.
5. Serve sprinkled with the ham.

Gurkensuppe
Cucumber Soup

This recipe comes from the Parkhotel Fürstenhof in Celle.

Serves 4

1 large cucumber
4 cups (1 litre) water or chicken stock
  (see p. 134)
¼ cup (1 oz) chopped spring onions
  (scallions)
½ clove garlic, finely chopped
30 g (1 oz) butter
¼ cup (1 oz) flour
1 teaspoon chopped fresh marjoram

1 teaspoon chopped fresh thyme
1 teaspoon chopped fresh basil
salt
freshly ground black pepper
pinch of nutmeg
½ cup (4 fl oz) fresh cream
4 tablespoons sour cream
fresh dill, finely chopped

1. Peel the cucumber and save the skins. Cut the cucumber lengthwise, and with a tablespoon remove and reserve the seeds.
2. In a saucepan, cook the peelings and the seeds in the water or chicken stock for approximately 45 minutes.
3. Cut the cucumber into slices. Sauté the cucumber with the spring onions and garlic in the butter, and sprinkle with flour.
4. Strain the stock over the sautéed cucumber and spring onions.
5. Add the marjoram, thyme, basil, salt and pepper and simmer for approximately 10 minutes.
6. Add the fresh cream and heat it but do not boil.
7. Cool the soup and refrigerate for 3 hours.
8. Serve in individual soup bowls with a tablespoon of sour cream and a sprinkling of dill.

Moselländische Sauerkrautsuppe
Sauerkraut Soup from the Moselle

This dish is a speciality of Alte Thorschenke in Cochem.

Serves 6

315 g (10 oz) fresh Sauerkraut
1 large onion, sliced
105 g (3½ oz) butter
4-6 cups (1-1.5 litres) beef stock
  (see p. 136)
1 teaspoon chopped fresh marjoram
  (or ¼ teaspoon dried)

1 teaspoon chopped fresh thyme (or ¼
  teaspoon dried)
1 clove garlic, crushed
freshly ground black pepper
salt
6 slices white bread, cut into cubes
½ cup (4 fl oz) sour cream

1. Place the Sauerkraut, onion and 45 g of the butter in a heavy-bottomed saucepan and simmer for 20 minutes.
2. Add the beef stock and continue to simmer for 1 hour.
3. Five minutes before completing the cooking, add the herbs, garlic and pepper. Taste before adding salt, as the Sauerkraut may have made it sufficiently salty.
4. Fry the bread in the remaining butter until golden brown.
5. Before serving, mix in the sour cream and serve the soup sprinkled with the fried bread.

Leberknödelsuppe
Liver Dumpling Soup

From the Posthotel Koblerbräu in Bad Tölz.

Serves 4-6

8 stale bread rolls, cut into slices
salt
1 cup (8 fl oz) lukewarm milk
250 g (8 oz) pork or beef liver, cut into
  cubes
1 small onion
½ clove garlic

1 sprig parsley
2 eggs, beaten
1 tablespoon finely chopped fresh
  marjoram
4 cups (1 litre) strong beef stock
  (see p. 136)

1. Place the bread roll slices and salt in the milk and soak for 5 minutes.
2. Squeeze out all the liquid and mix together the bread rolls, liver, onion, garlic and parsley. Put this mixture through a meat grinder or food processor.
3. Add the eggs and marjoram and, using floured hands, make small dumplings.
4. Heat the beef stock, place the dumplings into it and cook for approximately 20 minutes. Season to taste and serve hot.

Fränkische Gemüsesuppe
Franconian Vegetable Soup

Any number or combination of vegetables in season may be used for this soup.

Serves 6

750 g (1½ lb) mixed vegetables, cut into
  small pieces
4 cups (1 litre) strong beef stock
  (see p. 136)
1 teaspoon chopped fresh mixed herbs
  in season

¼ cup (2 fl oz) sour cream
salt
freshly ground black pepper

1. Place the vegetables in the stock, beginning with those that require longer cooking and adding the others at intervals. Simmer gently for 15 to 30 minutes, depending upon the vegetables chosen.
2. Before serving, mix in the herbs and sour cream. Season and serve hot.

Burg Elz

The castle Burg Elz is one of the most fascinating and romantic of all German fairytale castles. Situated in one of the many tranquil side valleys of the Moselle, it has been in the possession of the Elz clan since the 12th Century.

Its unusual, broken-up character is due to the fact that several branches of the family were living there, each in its own house.

Steep roofs, towers, chimneys and dormer windows give the castle an attractive picturebook silhouette.

The dream-like setting, on a knoll in a narrow wooded valley, contributes to make Burg Elz one of the most photographed, painted, universally well-known and beloved castles in the country. Only a footway leads through the ancient, mysterious forest from the little town of Moselkern an der Mosel.

The castle is beautifully preserved and maintained. A visit there many years ago has remained one of the memorable experiences of my childhood.

Königsberger Kohlsuppe
Cabbage Soup

Serves 6

2 pig's trotters
2 calf's knuckles
1 ham bone or bacon bones
6 cups (1.5 litres) water
2 tablespoons vinegar
500 g (1 lb) white cabbage, roughly
   chopped
250 g (8 oz) parsnip, sliced

250 g (8 oz) potatoes, peeled and cut
   into small dice
½ teaspoon caraway seeds, crushed
salt
freshly ground black pepper
1 cup (8 fl oz) sour cream
3 sprigs parsley, finely chopped

1. Place trotters, knuckles and ham bone in a large saucepan, add water and bring to the boil. Simmer for 2 hours.
2. Half-fill a separate saucepan with water and bring it to the boil. Add the vinegar and cabbage, and cook for 2 minutes. Drain and set aside.
3. Remove trotters, knuckles and ham bone from the stock, cool the stock and de-grease it. Cut off all the meat from the bones, chop it and set it aside.
4. To the stock add the cabbage, parsnips and potatoes and simmer for 30 minutes.
5. Add caraway seeds, salt, pepper and chopped meat. Stir in the sour cream and serve sprinkled with parsley.

Grüne Erbsensuppe mit Saurer Sahne
Pea Soup with Sour Cream

Serves 4-6

250 g (8 oz) fresh shelled peas
2 cups (16 fl oz) chicken stock
   (see p. 134)
90 g (3 oz) butter, softened
2 tablespoons flour
1 egg yolk

½ cup (4 fl oz) sour cream
salt
freshly ground black pepper
4 slices white bread, cubed
2 tablespoons chopped chives

1. Cook the peas in the stock for 10 to 15 minutes or until soft.
2. Rub them through a sieve, or purée in a food processor or blender.
3. Make a paste from half the butter, the flour, egg yolk and sour cream.
4. Mix the pea purée and the paste together. Heat but do not boil. Season.
5. Make sippets by frying the bread cubes in the remaining butter until golden.
6. Serve the soup hot with the sippets and sprinkled with chives.

Brotsuppe
Franconian Bread Soup

Serves 6

6 slices stale Pumpernickel or rye
   bread
8 cups (2 litres) beef stock (see p. 136)
1 onion, chopped
2 tablespoons lard

¼ cup (2 fl oz) sour cream
salt
freshly ground black pepper

1. Cut the bread into small pieces and add the heated beef stock. Allow to stand until the bread softens.
2. Sauté the onion in the lard until it is soft and golden brown, then add it to the bread and stock and simmer for 30 minutes.
3. Add the sour cream and season to taste.

Siegerländer Käsesuppe

Cheese Soup from Siegerland

This recipe comes from the Hotel Kaisergarten in Siegen.

Today Siegen is a modern town, but its origins are medieval and many of the old houses and churches are still preserved. Siegen's main claim to fame is that it is the birthplace of Reubens, and its art gallery contains several of his paintings. The Hotel Kaisergarten is part of modern Siegen, and while the town is not known as a great gourmet centre, very good food is served in some of its restaurants. Except for the Siegerlander Käsesuppe, a very tasty local cheese soup, most of the food served at the Hotel Kaisergarten is 'international'.

Serves 4

2 onions, cut into julienne strips
60 g (2 oz) butter
1 tablespoon flour
4 cups (1 litre) beef stock (see p. 136)
4 tablespoons grated Gruyère cheese

2 egg yolks
salt
freshly ground black pepper
⅛ teaspoon nutmeg
4 tablespoons sour cream

1. Lightly sauté the onions in the butter, and when light brown, sprinkle with flour.
2. Heat the beef stock and slowly pour it over the onions, stirring constantly.
3. In a separate saucepan, melt the grated cheese over low heat. Remove from the flame and mix in the egg yolks.
4. Combine the cheese with the onions and beef stock, season lightly with salt and pepper and add the nutmeg.
5. Serve in soup bowls and garnish each one with a tablespoon of sour cream.

Kraftbrühe 'Kaiserworth'

Consommé 'Kaiserworth'
This recipe comes from the Hotel Kaiserworth in Goslar.

Serves 4

4 cups (1 litre) strong-flavoured
  chicken stock (see p. 134)
1 leek, white part only, cut into
  julienne strips
1 carrot, cut into julienne strips
2 stalks celery, cut into julienne strips
pinch of nutmeg

salt
freshly ground black pepper
1 teaspoon finely chopped herbs
¾ cup (3 oz) flour
1 egg
¾-1 cup (6-8 fl oz) milk
butter

1. Put the chicken stock into a saucepan, add the vegetables, nutmeg, salt, pepper and herbs and simmer for 5 minutes, making sure that the vegetables are not over-cooked.
2. From the flour, egg and milk make a pancake batter. Cook the pancakes in butter in a frying pan.
3. When the pancakes have cooled down, fold them in half and cut them into thin strips.
4. To serve, place some strips of pancake into each soup bowl and pour the consommé and vegetables over them.

Fischsuppe 'Cuxhaven'
Cuxhaven Fish Soup

Serves 6-8

60 g (2 oz) butter
315 g (10 oz) potatoes, peeled and cut
  into cubes
1 carrot, cut into cubes
2 onions, chopped
2 stalks celery, chopped
1 leek, white part only, chopped

6 sprigs parsley, chopped
salt
freshly ground black pepper
6 cups (1.5 litres) fish stock (see p. 137)
500 g (1 lb) any white-fleshed fish, cut
  into chunks

1. In a large saucepan, heat the butter and lightly sauté all the vegetables and parsley. Season with salt and pepper.
2. Add the fish stock and cook for 15 minutes.
3. Add the fish and simmer lightly for 5 minutes. Serve immediately.

Muschelsuppe
Mussel Soup

Serves 4

1 kg (2 lb) mussels in the shell
¼ cup (2 fl oz) water
3 slices bacon, finely chopped
2 onions, chopped
1 stalk celery, chopped

3 potatoes, peeled and diced
salt
freshly ground black pepper
2 cups (16 fl oz) milk

1. Thoroughly clean the mussels and place them in a large saucepan with the water. Cover and cook briefly until the shells open.
2. Take the mussels out of the shells and chop them coarsely.
3. In a heavy-bottomed frying pan, fry the bacon. Add the onions and celery, and sauté lightly. Add the potatoes, salt and pepper and the remainder of the mussel cooking liquid
4. Cook for 15 to 20 minutes or until the potatoes are tender.
5. Stir in the milk and the chopped mussels. Heat through and serve.

Hamburger Aalsuppe
Hamburg Eel Soup

Serves 6

1 kg (2 lb) fresh eel, cut into 5 cm (2 in)
  pieces
6 cups (1.5 litres) fish stock (see p. 137)
1 tablespoon vinegar
salt
freshly ground black pepper
1 leek, white part only, chopped
1 carrot, diced
1 celery stalk, diced

1 cup (3 oz) small flowerets of
  cauliflower
1 cup (4 oz) shelled peas
2 tablespoons chopped parsley
1 cup (8 fl oz) white wine
1 can (approximately 410 g (13 oz)) pear
  halves, drained
2 tablespoons chopped parsley for
  garnish

1. Simmer the eel in the fish stock together with the vinegar, salt and pepper for approximately 10 to 15 minutes, or until it is tender.
2. Remove the eel from the stock and set aside.
3. To the fish stock add the vegetables, parsley and wine. Cook until the vegetables are soft.
4. Return the eel to the stock and add the pears. Heat without boiling.
5. Serve the soup sprinkled with chopped parsley.

Opposite: Some of the specialities of the Burghotel.
Clockwise from bottom left: Sorrel Soup; Saddle of Hare à la
Graf Reinhard; Red Cabbage with Apple (see p. 42);
Plum Compote.

Burghotel Sababurg

The Burghotel is also called Dornröschenschloss which means the Castle of the Sleeping Princess, and it is said to be the setting of the Brothers Grimm fairytale. The castle was built at the beginning of the fourteenth century and is situated in the Reinhardswald, one of Germany's largest forests. Needless to say, the restaurant specialises in all types of game. The forest abounds in deer, wild pig, hare and pheasant, and the chef has a large repertoire of traditional recipes.

Krebssuppe
Freshwater Crayfish Soup

Lobster, crayfish or prawns may be used in this recipe.

Serves 4-6

SOUP
6 slices stale white bread, crusts removed
4 cups (1 litre) milk
salt
1 teaspoon sugar
crayfish butter (see below)
4 cooked crayfish tails, sliced
60 g (2 oz) butter
¼ cup finely chopped parsley

CRAYFISH BUTTER
10 cooked crayfish tails, chopped
90 g (3 oz) butter
2 tablespoons chopped chives
2 tablespoons chopped celery
2 tablespoons chopped parsley
salt
freshly ground black pepper
1 teaspoon paprika pepper

Soup
1. Cut 3 of the slices of bread into small pieces and soak them in milk for 30 minutes.
2. Place the bread and milk in a saucepan and add the salt. Bring to the boil and boil for 5 minutes, stirring constantly. Add the sugar and cool the liquid.
3. Add the crayfish butter and place the liquid, 2 cups at a time, into a food processor or blender and purée until the liquid is smooth. Refrigerate for 3 to 4 hours.
4. Add the sliced crayfish tails.
5. Cut the remaining slices of bread into small cubes and fry them in the butter until they are golden brown sippets.
6. To serve, place the sippets in each bowl of soup and sprinkle with parsley.

Crayfish Butter
1. In a food processor or blender, combine all the ingredients and purée until they are smooth in texture.
2. Pass the crayfish butter through a sieve.

Berliner Nudelsuppe
Chicken Noodle Soup

Serves 6-8

1 small chicken (1.25 kg/2½ lb)
1 leek, chopped
3 stalks celery, chopped
2 carrots, sliced
1 onion, roughly chopped
12 peppercorns
3 bay leaves
8 cups (2 litres) water
100 g (3½ oz) soup egg noodles of your choice
salt
4 sprigs parsley, finely chopped

1. Place the chicken, leek, celery, carrots, onion, peppercorns and bay leaves into a large saucepan.
2. Add the water, slowly bring to the boil and simmer gently for 1 hour.
3. Remove the chicken and allow it to cool. Cut off all the meat from the bones and chop it into small pieces. Set aside. Remove the vegetables from the pan and set aside. Strain and de-grease the stock.
4. Add the noodles to the stock and boil over medium heat for 10 to 15 minutes until the noodles are soft and cooked.
5. Add the chopped chicken meat and vegetables and heat for 2 to 3 minutes. Season to taste.
6. Serve hot in soup bowls, making sure that each portion contains vegetables and meat. Sprinkle with parsley.

Kalbshirn Suppe
Calf's Brain Soup

This recipe comes from the Hotel Bayerischer Hof in Lindau im Bodensee.

Serves 6

1 calf's brain
4 cups (1 litre) water
salt
1 tablespoon white wine vinegar
1 tablespoon finely chopped parsley
1 onion, chopped
60 g (2 oz) butter

¾ cup (3 oz) flour
¼ cup (2 fl oz) dry white wine
4 cups (1 litre) beef stock (see p. 136)
¼ cup (2 fl oz) sour cream
freshly ground black pepper
¼ teaspoon nutmeg

1. Rinse the brain under running water. Boil the water, salt and vinegar and blanch the brain for about 5 minutes.
2. Lightly sauté the parsley and onion in the butter and add the flour, stirring constantly. Heat the white wine and pour it over the flour mixture. Add the heated beef stock and stir to make sure that there are no lumps.
3. Bring to the boil, then reduce the heat. Add the roughly chopped brain, sour cream, salt, pepper, and nutmeg. Serve hot.

Apfelsuppe
Cold Apple Soup

Serves 6

750 g (1½ lb) apples, peeled and cut into
   small pieces
3 cups (24 fl oz) water
small piece lemon rind
juice of 1 lemon

¼ cup (2 oz) sugar
1 cup (8 fl oz) dry white wine
1 tablespoon cornflour (cornstarch)
⅓ cup (2 oz) raisins or sultanas

1. In a saucepan, combine the apples, water, lemon rind, lemon juice, sugar and white wine, and cook until the apples are soft.
2. Purée the apples with the liquid in a blender or food processor.
3. Return the soup to the saucepan and bring to the boil. Add the cornflour (which has been mixed with a little water), and simmer gently until the soup thickens. (The flavour may be adjusted by the addition of further sugar and/or lemon juice.)
4. Add the raisins, cool the soup, refrigerate and serve icy cold.

Weinsuppe
Wine Soup

This soup may be made with white wine, in which case lemon rind and lemon juice are used; or with red wine, in which case cinnamon and cloves can be added. The soup may be served hot, or icy cold.

Serves 6

2 egg yolks
¼-⅓ cup (2-3 oz) sugar
1 tablespoon cornflour (cornstarch),
   dissolved in ¼ cup (2 fl oz) water
3 cups (24 fl oz) dry white or red wine

1 cup (8 fl oz) water
grated lemon rind
juice 1 lemon
pinch powdered cinnamon
2-3 cloves

1. Cream the egg yolks with the sugar until the sugar has dissolved. Add the cornflour, wine and water. If you're using white wine, add lemon rind and juice; with the red wine add cinnamon and cloves.
2. Place the saucepan on a gentle flame, and with a whisk continue beating the mixture until it fluffs up. Be careful not to overheat, as the egg yolk may set.
3. The flavour may be adjusted by adding more lemon juice and/or sugar.

Vegetables

The German kitchen has its own particular way of dealing with vegetables and while any variety is available, by popular choice the repertoire is limited.

The potato undoubtedly heads the list and while it is said that a whole book could be filled with Irish potato recipes, I personally think that the Germans could muster a greater number.

The different varieties of cabbage follow closely in popularity and it is amazing in just how many ways German cooks can transform the humble and basically boring cabbage into delicious fragrant dishes.

Germany, of course, is famous for its Sauerkraut and here again many ingenious ways of preparing it result in that tasty, very German, flavour. They even make a Sauerkrautkuchen, a sort of pie. Sauerkraut itself is simply made by finely shredding the cabbage and pickling it in stone jars or wooden barrels, alternating layers of cabbage and salt and covering the top with muslin. A weight is then put on top.

Sauerkraut should be pickled in approximately 2 weeks.

Asparagus is highly regarded and is considered an aristocrat of vegetables. In springtime during its short season it is eagerly sought out, not only for immediate consumption but also for preserving, to be served during the winter.

The Germans have an original and unusual way of combining vegetables and fruit. In Birnen, Bohnen und Speck, a Westphalian speciality, pears, green beans and heavy smoked Speck are cooked in a sour sauce.

Blindes Huhn has nothing to do with a blind chicken but is a mixture of carrots and green beans with bacon and apples, while Himmel und Erde (Heaven and Earth) is mashed potatoes and apples sometimes served with onions, blood sausage or bacon.

In the winter dried peas, beans and lentils are incoporated in many tasty dishes such as Swabian lentils or Berliner pea purée.

There is a very strong tradition of vegetable home preserving, an art which is slowly disappearing because of the availability of canned vegetables in supermarkets.

Spargel Freiburg
Freiburg Asparagus

Serves 6

1 kg (2 lb) fresh asparagus
90 g (3 oz) butter

⅓ cup (3 oz) grated Parmesan cheese
1 egg, hard-boiled

1. Cut off the ends of the asparagus and, if necessary, peel the tough skin.
2. The asparagus may be boiled in salted water for 7 to 8 minutes or steamed in a special asparagus steamer.
3. Heat the butter until it turns light brown. Remove from the flame and add the cheese. Spoon this mixture over the asparagus.
4. Finely chop the hard-boiled egg and sprinkle it on top of the butter and cheese sauce. Serve immediately.

Himmel und Erde ('Heaven and Earth')
Puréed Potatoes and Apples with Black Pudding

One of the most famous traditional Rhineland dishes.

Serves 4

4 large potatoes, peeled and diced
3 cooking apples, peeled, cored
  and quartered
salt

freshly ground black pepper
1 tablespoon sugar
75 g (2½ oz) butter
500 g (1 lb) Blutwurst (black pudding)

1. In a saucepan, cook the potatoes in salted water for 15 minutes.
2. Drain off most of the water and add the apples. Cook until tender.
3. Mash the potato and apple mixture, and season with the salt and pepper. Add the sugar and 60 g of the butter.
4. Slice the Blutwurst and fry in the remaining butter until brown on each side.
5. To serve, arrange the fried slices of sausage over the mashed potato and apple mixture.

Bayerische Kartoffelklösse
Bavarian Potato Dumplings

Serve these instead of potatoes with any main course. From the Goldene Sonne in Landshut.

Makes 12-15 dumplings

10 large potatoes
2 bread rolls
60 g (2 oz) butter or lard
3 eggs
salt

freshly ground black pepper
½ teaspoon nutmeg
8 cups (2 litres) beef stock (see p. 136)
  or salted water

1. Cook the potatoes until they are quite soft. Cool and grate them on a metal grater.
2. Cut the bread rolls into cubes and fry them in the butter or lard.
3. Place the grated potatoes in a mixing bowl and mix together with the eggs, salt, pepper and nutmeg. Add the fried bread cubes.
4. With floured hands, form the dumplings.
5. Place them in gently boiling stock or salted water and cook for approximately 10 minutes. Leave them in the water for a further 5 minutes, then drain in a colander.

Saure Meerrettichkartoffeln

Sour Horse-radish Potatoes

A very tasty way of giving potatoes a new and interesting flavour. Dill, marjoram or parsley may be used instead of horse-radish.

Serves 4-6

6 medium-sized potatoes, peeled and
   cut into 6 mm (¼ in) slices
2 cups (16 fl oz) milk or beef stock
   (see p. 136)
salt
freshly ground black pepper
75 g (2½ oz) Speck or smoked bacon,
   finely diced

¼ cup (1 oz) flour
1½ tablespoons wine or cider vinegar
3 tablespoons prepared horse-radish
½ teaspoon sugar
3 tablespoons sour cream (optional)
2 sprigs parsley, finely chopped

1. Boil the potatoes in milk with salt and pepper until they are soft.
2. Drain and reserve the milk.
3. Place the potatoes in a glass or china serving dish and keep warm while preparing the sauce.
4. In a heavy frying pan fry the Speck or bacon until it is crisp and golden.
5. Stir in the flour and cook on a low heat until the flour is light blond colour.
6. Slowly add the hot milk and stir to a thick, smooth consistency.
7. Add the vinegar and simmer for 5 minutes.
8. Add horse-radish and sugar and, for a richer sauce, the sour cream. Heat but do not boil. Season.
9. Pour the sauce over the potatoes and mix in gently. Serve sprinkled with parsley as a vegetable accompanying sausages and smoked meat cuts.

Schmorkraut

Braised Fresh Cabbage

Serves 4-6

1 kg (2 lb) head of green cabbage
60 g (2 oz) Speck or smoked bacon,
   diced
salt
freshly ground black pepper
3 tablespoons tomato paste

1-1½ cups (8-12 fl oz) stock or water
30 g (1 oz) butter
¼ cup (1 oz) fine dry breadcrumbs
juice of 1 lemon
¼ cup (1 oz) grated Parmesan-type
   cheese

1. Cut the cabbage into 6 or 8 wedges, remove the core, wash and drain well.
2. In a heavy-bottomed, lidded saucepan, melt the Speck or bacon.
3. Add the cabbage wedges and brown them gently. Season.
4. In a bowl dissolve the tomato paste in the stock or water and gradually, over a period of 45 minutes to an hour, add this liquid to the saucepan. (The liquid should only cover the bottom of the saucepan.) To obtain best results keep the heat low and the lid on. Turn the cabbage occasionally.
5. To serve, arrange the cabbage wedges on a serving dish and pour any remaining cooking liquid over them. Keep hot.
6. Heat the butter and fry the breadcrumbs until they are crisp.
7. Sprinkle the cabbage with lemon juice, breadcrumbs and cheese and serve hot.

Rotkohl
Red Cabbage and Apples

Serves 4-6

45 g (1½ oz) butter
500-750 g (1-1½ lb) red cabbage,
  shredded
juice 1 lemon

2 apples, peeled and diced
2 tablespoons red currant jelly
2 cloves
2 tablespoons beef stock (see p. 136)

1. In a heavy-bottomed casserole melt the butter. Add the cabbage and pour over the lemon juice (this will help to preserve the colour). Add the apples, red currant jelly, cloves and beef stock.
2. Mix all the ingredients together and simmer for 10 to 20 minutes. The cabbage should not be over-cooked.

Freiburg im Breisgau, Schwarzwald

When I first saw Freiburg some 2-3 years after the Second World War, the town centre surrounding the cathedral was in ruins. Destroyed were the beautiful ancient mediaeval buildings which once gave the city its great charm. The Freiburger Münster, its superb Gothic cathedral was badly damaged, the once famous colourful leaded windows gaping.

When I returned in summer of 1979, I was gratified to find a town rebuilt, the cathedral and some of its most valuable historical buildings restored to their former glory. Alas some of its original charm and character was lost forever.

Today, as for hundreds of years, the cathedral with its lace-like tower dominates the townscape and the life still revolves around the square which surrounds the venerable church. Here the ancient and the modern placed next to each other symbolise the spirit which is so evident throughout the country; the spirit which made it possible to heal the wounds and to permit the people to create a new life rising out of the ruins.

Freiburg, once the epitome of olden times, is today a thoroughly modern city. Its attractive setting in the landscape, surrounded by the distant hills of the Black Forest makes it a popular centre of the arts, commerce and education. It's a convenient starting point for the gratifying exploration of the southern parts of the Black Forest.

Schwäbisches Sauerkraut
Swabian Sauerkraut

Serves 6

1 kg (2 lb) fresh Sauerkraut
3 apples, peeled and diced
1 onion, sliced
2 tablespoons lard
½ teaspoon crushed juniper berries

1 teaspoon sugar
2 tablespoons flour
2 cups (16 fl oz) dry white wine
½ teaspoon salt
freshly ground black pepper

1. Sauerkraut may be bought in tins or in bulk. For best results, rinse the Sauerkraut in warm water and drain well.
2. Sauté the apples and onions in the lard until light brown. Add the juniper berries, sugar and Sauerkraut. Cover and simmer for 30 minutes.
3. Add the flour and stir in well, then add the wine, salt and pepper. Continue simmer for approximately 1 hour until the Sauerkraut is tender.

Note: Sauerkraut may be served with Spätzle (see p. 140).

Linsen auf Schwäbische Art
Swabian Lentils

Serves 6

3 onions, sliced
3 slices bacon, diced
500 g (1 lb) lentils
2 carrots, peeled and diced
155 g (5 oz) ham, diced
315 g (10 oz) left-over meat (pork, beef or veal), diced

4 cups (1 litre) water
2 teaspoons salt
freshly ground black pepper
4 frankfurters, sliced
2 cups cooked Spätzle (see p. 140)
1 tablespoon chopped parsley
vinegar

1. Sauté the onions and bacon until the onions are soft. Add the lentils, carrots, ham and cooked left-over meat.
2. Cover with water and salt. Cook, covered, for 1½ hours, adding more water if necessary.
3. When the lentils are cooked, taste for seasoning.
4. Add the frankfurters and Spätzle. Simmer for 5 minutes.
5. Serve sprinkled with parsley and a dash of vinegar.

Westfälische Dicke Bohnen
Westphalian Broadbeans

Serves 4

1 kg (2 lb) broadbeans
salt
100 g (3½ oz) Speck or smoked bacon,
  diced

freshly ground black pepper
3 sprigs parsley, finely chopped
2 sprigs marjoram, finely chopped

1. Shell the beans and cook them in salted water for 20 minutes, drain.
2. Fry the Speck or bacon until the fat is rendered and the meat is crisp but not burnt.
3. In a serving dish mix the beans with the Speck or bacon. Add salt and pepper and toss them with parsley and marjoram.
4. Serve hot with mashed potatoes.

Berliner Linsentopf
Lentils with Bacon

Serves 6

375 g (12 oz) green lentils, soaked
  overnight
5 cups (1.25 litres) beef stock
  (see p. 136)
2 potatoes, diced
3 tablespoons vinegar
3 tablespoons sugar

salt
freshly ground black pepper
250 g (8 oz) smoked Speck or bacon,
  chopped
2 onions, finely chopped
3 tablespoons finely chopped parsley

1. In a heavy-bottomed saucepan, cook the lentils in the beef stock for 45 minutes.
2. Add the potatoes and cook for a further 15 minutes.
3. Add the vinegar, sugar, salt and pepper.
4. In a frying pan, melt and brown the Speck or bacon. Add the onions and fry lightly.
5. Add the Speck, onions and parsley to the lentils and mix well. Serve hot as a vegetable with meat.

Süss-Saure Grüne Bohnen

Sweet-Sour Beans

Serves 4

500 g (1 lb) stringless beans cut into
    5 cm (2 in) lengths
2 cups (16 fl oz) beef stock (see p. 136)
salt
freshly ground black pepper
60 g (2 oz) butter

1 tablespoon flour
juice 1 lemon
1 teaspoon white wine vinegar
1 tablespoon sugar
1 onion, chopped

1. In a saucepan, cook the beans in the beef stock together with the salt and pepper for approximately 15 minutes.
2. Soften 45 g of the butter and mix it with the flour, then add to the beans and beef stock.
3. Add the lemon juice, vinegar and sugar and mix well.
4. In the remaining butter, lightly fry the onions and add them to the beans. Cook this mixture for a further 15 minutes.
5. Traditionally these beans are served with pork dishes.

Berliner Erbsenpüree

Berlin Pea Purée

This is served as a vegetable accompanying meat dishes.

Serves 4-6

500 g (1 lb) dried yellow peas, soaked
    overnight
2 onions, chopped

60 g (2 oz) bacon, chopped
salt
freshly ground black pepper

1. Drain the peas and place them in a heavy-bottomed saucepan. Cover with fresh water and cook slowly until the peas are soft. Drain them, reserving ½ cup of the liquid.
2. In a frying pan, fry the onions with the bacon.
3. Add the onions and bacon to the peas and season with salt and pepper.
4. One cup at a time, place the peas in a food processor and purée. Add some of the reserved liquid if the purée is too thick.

Birnen, Bohnen und Speck

Pears, Beans and Bacon

A speciality of Westphalia

Serves 6

6 ripe pears, peeled and sliced
½ teaspoon grated lemon rind
½ cup water
1 teaspoon salt
6 slices bacon or heavy smoked Speck

¼ cup (2 oz) sugar
2 tablespoons vinegar
1 teaspoon lemon juice
500 g (1 lb) green beans, cut into 2.5 cm
    (1 in) lengths

1. In a saucepan cook the pear slices and lemon rind in the water for 10 minutes.
2. Meanwhile chop the bacon and fry it in a pan until it is crisp. Remove and drain on absorbent paper.
3. Add the sugar, vinegar and lemon juice to the bacon fat. Cook for 3 minutes.
4. Add the beans and salt to the pears and pour this sauce over them. Continue cooking until tender.
5. Just before serving, add the crisp pieces of bacon to the beans and pears. Serve as a vegetable dish.

*Opposite Top: Some of the food offered by Schloss Saaleck.
From left: Sugared Berries with Cream; Smoked Trout;
Crumbed Pork Chops with Rémoulade Sauce.*

Hotel Schloss Saaleck, Hammelburg

Schloss Saaleck is one of many old German castles which in recent years have been transformed into elegant comfortable hotels.
Saaleck is situated high above the valley of the Saale river, it commands a beautiful view of the surrounding hills and forests. The food there is simple country fare and occasionally game and local river trout are offered. The wines are from their own cellars.

Historische Wurstküche, Regensburg

The Historical Sausage Kitchen is a very simple restaurant set in a small old building beside the fast-flowing Danube. The seating consists of benches sheltered by striped canvas awnings and large sun umbrellas.
Spicy local sausages are fried in the tiny, smoky kitchen, which provides 'no-nonsense' service. A glass of beer invariably accompanies the delicious feast of sausages, Sauerkraut and potato salad.

Schmorgurken
Stewed Cucumbers with Sour Cream and Dill

Serves 6

1.5 kg (3 lb) fresh cucumbers
1 teaspoon salt
30 g (1 oz) butter
60 g (2 oz) onions, finely chopped
1½ tablespoons flour
1¾ cups (14 fl oz) milk

1½ tablespoons sour cream
1 tablespoon chopped parsley
1 tablespoon chopped dill
salt
freshly ground pepper

1. Peel the cucumbers, cut them in half lengthways, and with a small spoon remove the seeds. Cut the halves crosswise into 2.5 cm (1 in) pieces.
2. Place them in a bowl and sprinkle with salt. Let the cucumber stand for 30 minutes then drain off the liquid.
3. In a frying pan, melt the butter, and sauté the onions until light brown. Add the flour and cook until the flour turns light brown.
4. Add the milk, stirring constantly and boil for 3 to 4 minutes.
5. Add the cucumbers and simmer for 10 to 15 minutes. The cucumber must be tender but still quite firm.
6. Add the sour cream, parsley and dill. Season to taste.

Leipziger Allerlei
Leipzig Mixed Vegetable Platter

Serves 6

250 g (8 oz) cauliflower, cut into
   flowerets
2 large carrots, diced
500 g (1 lb) shelled green peas (buy
   1 kg (2 lb) fresh peas)

250 g (8 oz) green beans, sliced
125 g (4 oz) button mushrooms
45 g (1½ oz) butter
¼ cup chopped parsley

1. The traditional recipe calls for the vegetables to be cooked in separate saucepans. However, if the vegetables are added at intervals, they can all be cooked in one saucepan.
2. Start with the cauliflower and carrots. Cook them in boiling salted water for 5 minutes, then add the peas and beans. Cook for a further 10 minutes or until the vegetables are cooked but still crisp. Drain, and save ½ cup of the liquid in which the vegetables have cooked.
3. Arrange the vegetables on a platter and keep them warm.
4. Sauté the mushrooms in the butter until they are light brown. Add them to the serving platter and sprinkle them with a little of the butter in which they were cooked. Pour the reserved liquid over them and sprinkle with the chopped parsley.

Blindes Huhn ('Blind Hen')
Carrots and Green Beans with Bacon and Apples

Serves 6

4 large carrots, diced
250 g (8 oz) green beans, cut into
   2.5 cm (1 in) pieces
3 slices bacon, diced
1 tablespoon butter
2 onions, sliced

3 cooking apples, peeled and sliced
1 tablespoon sugar
2 tablespoons white wine vinegar
salt
freshly ground black pepper

1. In a saucepan, cook the carrots and beans in salted water until they are almost tender. Drain and set the vegetables aside.
2. Sauté the bacon in the butter until crisp. them remove and set aside.
3. Cook the onions in the bacon fat and butter until they are soft but not brown. Add the apples, sugar and vinegar and the partially cooked carrots and beans. Add the crisp bacon and season.
4. Cover and cook until the vegetables are heated through.

Semmelknödel
Bread Roll Dumplings

This recipe comes from the Schlosshotel in Hochenschwangau. They can be served instead of potatoes with a main course dish.

Makes 12-15

8-10 stale bread rolls
2 cups (16 fl oz) milk, warmed
salt
1 tablespoon lard

1 small onion, finely chopped
3 tablespoon finely chopped parsley
3-4 eggs

1. Cut the bread rolls into slices and place them in the lukewarm milk and salt for 20 to 30 minutes.
2. Squeeze out all the liquid and place the bread rolls in a mixing bowl.
3. Melt the lard in a frying pan and lightly sauté the onions and parsley. Add them to the bread rolls. Mix in the eggs and form the dough into dumplings.
4. Bring enough salted water to the boil to cover the dumplings and carefully place the dumplings into it. Simmer for 15 to 20 minutes.
5. Remove the dumplings from the water with a slotted spoon and place them in a colander to drain.

Fish

The most popular of German freshwater fish is trout and the most popular way to eat it is blau. Germans will go to a great deal of trouble to arrange tanks full of trout so that they can be caught and cooked while they're absolutely fresh.

Blaue Forelle or blue trout gets its name from the colour of its skin which turns a steely blue only when freshly cooked in a stock which contains vinegar among other ingredients. The colouring will occur only if the fish is completely fresh and the fine film of slime which covers the fish is undisturbed. Nothing else is done in this classic preparation and the trout is served hot with melted butter, lemon juice, boiled potatoes and a lettuce salad. Simple but without comparison!

Salmon, now very rare and expensive, as well as carp are also prepared blau.

In general fish boiled or poached in an aromatic court bouillon is more popular than fried fish.

Modern transport makes freshwater fish available along the seashores while seafish is eaten fresh in the most remote corners of the country.

In the north, fish stews and casseroles are popular and, as in the bouillabaisse of Marseilles, the German cooks use whatever fresh fish is available in the day's catch.

Sole, halibut and turbot are held in high esteem and have always graced elegant German dinner tables.

Lobster, crayfish and prawns or shrimp, while very expensive are the pride of many fine German restaurants, prepared in accordance with old, well-tried recipes.

The list of freshwater fish is long, at the top the noble Forelle (trout), closely followed by the ever-popular pike and carp. Eel is eaten fresh or smoked. The experience of eating small tender young eel, freshly smoked as presented at the Spieker in Bad Zwischenahn is not easily forgotten.

Freshwater crayfish, now a rarity and mostly imported, are a great delicacy when served in a cream and dill sauce.

Herrings are ever-present in all parts of Germany and are eaten in a variety of dishes, fresh or pickled, salted, sweet or sour; the Germans love them.

While most of the fish dishes in Germany are fairly elaborate, often served in rich and spicy sauces, Blaue Forelle is still top favourite!

A typical German way to serve trout: Trout Fillets in Aspic.

Hamburger Fischgericht
Fish Stew

Serves 6

750 g (1½ lb) fish fillets, cut into 2-3 cm
  (1-1½ in) pieces
juice of 1 lemon
salt
freshly ground black pepper
2 teaspoons paprika
45 g (1½ oz) butter or Speck, diced

2 onions, finely chopped
3 sprigs parsley, finely chopped
500 g (1 lb) potatoes, peeled and sliced
3 eggs, lightly beaten
¾ cup (6 fl oz) sour cream
¾ cup (6 fl oz) yoghurt

1. Preheat oven to 180°C (350°F/Gas 4).
2. Place the fish pieces in a dish and sprinkle them with lemon juice, salt, pepper and paprika. Allow to stand for 30 minutes.
3. Heat the butter or melt the Speck, and sauté the onions and parsley until the onions are soft and transparent.
4. In a deep greased casserole, place the fish pieces, onion and potato slices in alternate layers.
5. In a bowl combine eggs, sour cream and yoghurt. Season.
6. Pour the mixture into the casserole, cover and bake for 30 minutes. Remove the lid and bake for a further 15 minutes.
7. Serve with a lettuce salad.

Nordsee Fischkasserolle
North Sea Fish Stew

This dish is very popular in Hamburg where fish available on the day is used.

Serves 6

45 g (1½ oz) butter
1 onion, chopped
500 g (1 lb) white-fleshed fish, cut into
  small cubes
250 g (8 oz) scallops
250 g (8 oz) fresh prawns (shrimps),
  shelled and cleaned
200 g (6½ oz) button mushrooms, sliced

1 cup (8 fl oz) fish stock (see p. 137)
1 cup (8 fl oz) dry white wine
½ teaspoon salt
freshly ground black pepper
2 cups (10 oz) cooked rice
1 tablespoon chopped parsley
3 tablespoons grated Parmesan cheese

1. Preheat the oven to 180°C (350°F/Gas 4).
2. In a heavy casserole, melt the butter and sauté the onion.
3. Add all the remaining ingredients except the Parmesan cheese and mix together well. Bake in the oven for 30 minutes.
4. Sprinkle with the cheese and place under the grill to brown.

Hamburger Fischpastete
Hamburg Seafood Pie

The traditional recipe calls for halibut and sole or flounder. If these two fish are not available, other similar fish may be used.

Serve 6 - 8

FILLING
1 kg (2 lb) halibut
500 g (1 lb) sole or flounder
1 carrot, chopped
1 stalk celery, chopped
1 onion, chopped
¼ cup chopped parsley
750 g (1½ lb) raw shelled prawns
   (shrimps)
1 can (approximately 400 g (12½ oz)
   asparagus tips, drained
60 g (2 oz) butter
3 tablespoons flour
¼ cup (2 fl oz) sour cream
1 egg yolk
salt
freshly ground black pepper

PASTRY
1 cup (4 oz) self-raising flour
¼ teaspoon salt
125 g (4 oz) butter
1 egg, beaten (reserve 1 teaspoon and
   mix with a few drops of water for
   glazing)
1 teaspoon grated lemon peel

Filling
1. Gently poach the fish in enough water to cover it, together with the carrot, celery, onion and parsley for 15 minutes. Cool the fish in the stock. When it is cold, remove the flesh from the bones. Discard the skin.
2. Strain the stock.
3. Add the prawns to the stock and simmer until they turn pink (approximately 2 to 3 minutes). Remove the prawns and save the stock.
4. Place the fish in a shallow ovenproof dish. Arrange the prawns and the asparagus tips on top.
5. Make a roux by melting the butter and adding the flour to it. Cook it for 4 to 5 minutes. Heat 2 cups of the fish stock and gradually add it to the roux. Cook for 5 to 10 minutes until the sauce is smooth and thick.
6. Beat the sour cream and the egg yolk together, add some of the hot sauce and then in turn pour the cream and yolk mixture back into the sauce. Season.
7. Pour the sauce over the fish in the ovenproof dish.

Pastry
1. Preheat the oven to 190°C (375°F/Gas 5).
2. Combine the flour and the salt. Chop the butter into small pieces and mix it with the flour until it resembles fine breadcrumbs. Add the egg and lemon peel and, with the minimum of kneading, prepare the dough.
3. Roll it out to the size of the ovenproof dish and lay it over the seafood mixture.
4. Brush the egg and water mixture over the pastry and bake the pie in the oven until the pastry is golden-brown and crisp.

Fisch in Backteig gebacken
Fried Fish in Beer Batter

Serves 6

6 large or 12 small fish fillets
juice of 1 lemon
salt
freshly ground black pepper
flour for dusting dish fillets
oil for frying
lemon wedges and parsley sprigs for
  garnish

BATTER
1¼ cups (5 oz) flour
1 cup (8 fl oz) beer
2 eggs, separated
2 teaspoons olive oil
salt

1. Arrange the fish fillets in a glass or china dish and sprinkle them with lemon juice, salt and pepper. Leave to stand for 30 minutes.
2. Prepare the batter by mixing all the ingredients except the egg whites to a smooth liquid consistency. Beat the egg whites until they are stiff and fold them into the batter.
3. Dust the fillets with the flour and dip them in the batter.
4. In a frying pan or deep fryer, preheat the oil and fry the fillets for 8 to 12 minutes until golden brown.
5. Drain them on a paper towel and serve hot, garnished with lemon wedges and parsley.

Hohenschwangau, Bavaria

The castle of Hohenschwangau and the nearby Neuschwanstein are the epitome of German romanticism. The first was built in 1832-36 by Maximilian II of Bavaria who was greatly influenced by English castles which served as a model. Maximilian's son Ludwig, spent many happy times as a youth at Hohenschwangau; he loved the fairytale-like setting and the breathtaking beauty of the surrounding countryside. The distant snow-covered peaks of the alps and the dark, mysterious and mist-shrouded nearby slopes appealed to his romantic and imaginative nature. His romantic mind was greatly stimulated by the music of Richard Wagner and when finally he set forth to create for himself the ultimate fantasy, he commissioned the famous stage designer, Christian Jank to design a fairytale dream castle.

Fisch auf Badische Art

Fish with Cheese and Tomato Sauce

Serves 4

750 g (1½ lb) fresh fish fillets such as
  snapper or bream
juice 1 lemon
salt
freshly ground black pepper
¾ cup (3 oz) grated Cheddar cheese
¼ cup (2 fl oz) sour cream

¼ cup (2 fl oz) milk
3 tablespoons chopped parsley
¼ cup (2 fl oz) tomato purée
20 g (¾ oz) butter, cut into pieces
2½ tablespoons dry breadcrumbs
1½ tablespoons grated Cheddar cheese
  for garnish.

1. Preheat the oven to 200°C (400°F/Gas 6).
2. Sprinkle the fish fillets with the lemon juice, salt and pepper and allow them to stand for 10 minutes.
3. Combine the grated cheese, sour cream, milk, salt, pepper, parsley and tomato purée and stir them into a smooth paste.
4. In a buttered fireproof glass or earthenware dish, arrange one layer of fish fillets.
5. Cover the fish with a layer of the cheese mixture, and continue with alternate layers, making sure to finish with a layer of the cheese mixture.
6. Place the dish in the oven, cover and cook for 10 to 15 minutes.
7. Remove from the oven, sprinkle with pieces of butter, breadcrumbs and cheese and return the dish, uncovered, to the oven for a further 15 minutes to brown the top. This can also be done under the grill.
8. Serve with a green salad.

Fischauflauf

Fish Soufflé

A food processor or mincer can be used in the preparation of this dish.

Serves 6

600 g (1⅓ lb) cooked fish fillets
3 stale bread rolls, soaked in water
1 onion, finely chopped
2 sprigs parsley, finely chopped
salt

freshly ground black pepper
1 cup (8 fl oz) sour cream
4 eggs, separated
3 anchovy fillets, cut into small pieces
½ cup (2 oz) grated Parmesan cheese

1. Preheat the oven to 200°C (400°F/Gas 6).
2. Mince the fish, bread rolls (well squeezed out), onion and parsley in the food processor or mincer.
3. Add the salt, pepper, sour cream and egg yolks.
4. Whip the egg whites until they are stiff and fold them into the mixture. Mix in the anchovies.
5. Pour the mixture into a buttered soufflé dish and bake for 30 to 40 minutes.
6. Sprinkle the top of the soufflé with the cheese 10 minutes before taking it out of the oven.
7. Serve hot with the salad of your choice.

Fischspeise mit Blumenkohl überbacken

Fish and Cauliflower Gratin

Serves 6

1 small cauliflower
salt
75 g (2½ oz) butter
⅓-½ cup (1½-2 oz) flour
2 cups (16 fl oz) fish stock, heated
  (see p. 137)
freshly ground black pepper
juice of 1 lemon
60 g (2 oz) Cheddar cheese, cut into
  small cubes

4 tablespoons cream
2 egg yolks
750 g (1½ lb) fish fillets, cut into 5 cm
  (2 in) pieces
2 tablespoons dry breadcrumbs
¼ cup (1 oz) grated Cheddar cheese,
  for topping

1. Preheat the oven to 200°C (400°F/Gas 6).
2. Divide the cauliflower into small flowerets and steam or boil them lightly so that they are still firm. If boiling, add salt to the water.
3. To prepare the sauce, melt 45 g of the butter and make a roux by adding the flour. Brown lightly, stirring constantly, and gradually add the hot fish stock. Season and cook for 10 minutes.
4. Remove the sauce from the heat and while still hot, beat in the cheese, cream and egg yolks. Do not cook this again.
5. In an ovenprooof dish, arrange the fish pieces and the cauliflower in layers.
6. Pour the sauce over the fish and cauliflower, sprinkle with breadcrumbs and dot with the remaining butter. Bake in the oven for 15 minutes.
7. Remove the dish from the oven and sprinkle it with grated cheese. Bake for a further 10 minutes to brown the cheese.
8. This dish may be served with parsley potatoes and a green salad.

Geräucherte Forelle Nach Art des Hauses

Smoked Trout

From the Hotel zur Alten Thorschenke in Cochem. Now that household-size smokers are available, this recipe is worth trying. The result is a very tasty smoked trout. No smoking time or method of smoking is given as instruction for the use of the individual smoker should be followed.

Serves 4

2 tablespoons coarse salt
3 tablespoons Worcestershire sauce
juice 1 lemon
2 fresh trout, weighing about
  375 g (12 oz) each, cleaned

½ cup chopped parsley
½ cup chopped watercress

1. Mix the salt, Worcestershire sauce and lemon juice and rub it all over the trout (inside and out).
2. Mix the parsley and watercress and place it inside the trout.
3. To smoke, follow the instructions attached to the smoker. Slow, cool smoking is recommended.
4. Traditionally the smoked trout is served with boiled parsley or dill potatoes and a salad made from sliced apples with a cream and horse-radish dressing.

Gesülzte Forellen
Jellied Trout

Serves 4

6 cups (1.5 litres) water
½ cup (4 fl oz) wine vinegar
salt
12 peppercorns
1 onion, chopped
3 bay leaves
3 stalks celery, chopped
1 cup (8 fl oz) dry white wine

4 small trout
6 teaspoons gelatine
2 egg whites, whipped
8 slices lemon
small sprigs parsley
1 egg, hard-boiled and sliced
1 tablespoon capers

1. In a fish kettle or large saucepan combine the water, vinegar, salt, peppercorns, onion, bay leaves, celery and white wine.
2. Bring to the boil and simmer for 30 minutes.
3. Reduce the heat, add the trout and cook slowly for 5 minutes. Cool the trout in the liquid.
4. Remove the trout and save the cooking liquid.
5. Cool the trout and carefully remove the flesh from the bones, in whole fillets on each side.
6. Arrange the fillets on a serving dish and refrigerate.
7. Strain the liquid and return it to the saucepan.
8. Heat it, and with a wire whisk mix the egg whites into it. Cook for 5 minutes. This will clarify the stock.
9. Filter the stock through a cloth and if necessary adjust the seasoning.
10. Remove 1 cup of the stock and dissolve the gelatine in it, then return it to the remaining stock, stirring well.
11. Decorate the top of the fillets and the serving dish with the lemon slices, parsley, hard-boiled egg and capers.
12. Carefully pour the liquid into the serving dish so that it covers the fish by 1 cm (½ in).
13. Refrigerate until the jelly sets and serve with mayonnaise (see p. 138) and salad.

Gefüllte Seezungenfilets
Stuffed Fillets of Sole

Serves 6

60 g (2 oz) butter
185 g (6 oz) shelled uncooked prawns (shrimps)
125 g (4 oz) cooked or canned crab, or lobster meat
2 tablespoons flour
1½ cups (12 fl oz) fish stock (see p. 137)
¼ cup (2 fl oz) fresh cream
2 tablespoons brandy

90 g (3 oz) button mushrooms, cut into slivers
½ cup (1 oz) fresh breadcrumbs
salt
freshly ground black pepper
6 or 12 sole fillets, depending on size (John Dory may be used)
4 tablespoons melted butter

1. Preheat the oven to 180°C (350°F/Gas 4).
2. In a saucepan, melt the butter and lightly sauté the prawns and the crab or lobster meat. Remove from the pan and set aside.
3. Add the flour to the butter in the pan, stir and cook for 3 minutes.
4. Slowly stir in the fish stock and then add the cream, brandy, mushrooms, breadcrumbs, prawns, crab, salt and pepper. Mix well together.
5. Allow the mixture to cool so that the sauce thickens.
6. Place an equal part of the stuffing on each fillet, roll it up, and secure it with a toothpick or some twine.
7. Brush the bottom of a baking dish with some of the melted butter.
8. Arrange the rolled fillets next to each other, and brush them with the melted butter.
9. Cover the dish with foil and bake it for 20 to 30 minutes. Serve hot from the baking dish.

Opposite: Some of the specialities of Heger's Parkhotel. Clockwise from bottom left: Roasted Pheasant with Grapes; Trout in Aspic; Saddle of Hare (see p. 88).

Heger's Parkhotel Flora, Schluchsee (Black Forest)

A journey through the Hochschwarzwald, the southern part of the Black Forest, is an unforgettable experience. It is easy to understand how the name originated. Dark, black-green conifer forests cover all mountainsides and most valleys; the twining roads pass through a few picturesque villages, but in general the feeling is one of lonely, serene mountain tranquillity.

The Schluchsee is one of a few mountain lakes, and the village high above its shores is a popular holiday resort.

Heger's Parkhotel is not only very attractive, but also contains a fine restaurant. Game from the local forests is a speciality. Pheasant with grapes appears on the menu, while saddle of hare is served larded with Speck in a cream sauce with juniper berries and cherries. There are also local edible snails which are cooked with white wine and lots of aromatic herbs in a delicious soup. The mountain streams are full of trout which Herr Heger serves in aspic.

The delightful setting of the restaurant which is surrounded by well-tended gardens, adds to the enjoyment of the good food.

Rheinsalm
Poached Rhine Salmon

Unfortunately there are hardly any fish left in the River Rhine and there are certainly no more salmon. Trout may be used as a substitute in this recipe (either a very large trout cut into 4 pieces, or 4 whole small trout).

Serves 4

2 cups (16 fl oz) dry white wine
1 cup (8 fl oz) water
1 onion, cut into small pieces
2 bay leaves
12 peppercorns
½ teaspoon salt

4 salmon steaks, 4 pieces of trout, or
  4 whole trout
1 cup (8 fl oz) cream
3 egg yolks, beaten
salt
freshly ground black pepper

1. Combine the wine, water, onion, bay leaves, peppercorns and salt and cook for approximately 10 minutes.
2. Reduce the heat and place the fish in the saucepan. Cover and simmer for approximately 10 minutes.
3. Remove the fish and keep warm.
4. Continue boiling the mixture until it is reduced to 1½ cups. Strain and return it to the rinsed-out pan.
5. Mix the cream and the egg yolks.
6. Using the whisk, beat a quarter of the reduced liquid into the egg mixture.
7. Place the saucepan on a low flame and mix in the rest of the liquid. Cook gently until the mixture thickens, making sure that it does not curdle. Season.
8. Serve the fish with the sauce poured over.

Matjesheringe in Rahmsosse
Matjes Herrings in Cream Sauce

Serves 6

8 herring fillets
1 cup (8 fl oz) buttermilk or milk
½ cup (4 fl oz) sour cream
¼ cup (2 fl oz) yoghurt
salt
freshly ground black pepper
1 teaspoon sugar

juice 1 lemon
1 onion, grated
1 tablespoon tomato purée
2 tablespoons prepared horse-radish
2 apples, peeled, cored and finely diced
1 sour cucumber, finely diced
2 tablespoons finely chopped dill

1. Place the fillets in the buttermilk for 2 to 3 hours. This will reduce the salty flavour of the herrings.
2. To prepare the cream sauce, combine the sour cream, yoghurt, salt and pepper, and whisk lightly.
3. Add the sugar, lemon juice, onion, tomato purée, horse-radish, apples and cucumber, and mix them thoroughly together.
4. The drained fillets cam be arranged whole or cut into pieces on a serving platter with the sauce poured over. Refrigerate for several hours before serving. and garnish with finely chopped dill.

Heilbutt Filet, Gebraten mit Steinpilzen, Tomaten und Artischoken
Halibut Fillet with Mushrooms, Tomatoes and Artichokes

A recipe from Waldschlösschen Bösehof in Bederkase.

Serves 4

4 fillets of halibut, flounder or John
   Dory
juice 1 lemon
salt
3 tablespoons flour
90 g (3 oz) butter
250 g (8 oz) mushrooms, sliced
4 artichoke hearts, cut in to quarters
½ cup (4 fl oz) demi-glace sauce
   (see p. 137)

⅓ cup chopped parsley
4 tomatoes, peeled and cut into small dice
4 potatoes, peeled and cut into small dice
⅓ cup (2½ fl oz) vegetable oil
freshly ground black pepper

1. Sprinkle the fillets with the lemon juice and salt and dust them with the flour.
2. In a frying pan, melt half the butter and fry the fillets lightly.
3. In a separate pan, fry the mushrooms and artichoke hearts in the remaining butter.
4. Add the demi-glace, parsley and tomatoes to the mushrooms and artichokes. Cook for about 5 minutes.
5. Fry the potatoes in a separate pan in the vegetable oil until they are crisp. Season.
6. To serve, arrange the fillets on plates and garnish with the mushroom and artichoke sauce. Serve the potatoes separately.

Gebratener Moselhecht

Baked Pike, Moselle Style

Serves 4

125 g (4 oz) butter
2 spring onions (scallions), chopped
1 carrot, finely diced
1 tablespoon chopped parsley
1 kg (2 lb) pike, or any available fish,
  cleaned

salt
1 cup (8 fl oz) fish stock (see p. 137)
½ cup (4 fl oz) sour cream
1 egg
½ cup (2 oz) grated Gruyère cheese

1. Preheat the oven to 180°C (350°F/Gas 4).
2. Using half the butter, grease a shallow baking tray. Scatter the vegetables and parsley on the bottom and place the fish on top of them. Sprinkle with salt, dot with the remaining butter and add the fish stock.
3. Cover the dish with foil and place it in the oven for 10 minutes.
4. Combine the sour cream and the egg. Remove the foil and spread the cream and egg mixture on top of the fish. Sprinkle with the cheese and increase the oven temperature to 200°C (400°F/Gas 6).
5. Return the dish to the oven and bake for a further 10 to 15 minutes.

Goslar

For hundreds of years the town of Goslar has played an important part in the history of Germany. In the Middle Ages it was the seat of German Emperors and was known as the northern Rome. Many old buildings bear witness to its illustrious past. Some 168 buildings which were built before 1580 remain, and at least 1000 are protected under the Preservation Act. Today only 10 of the 47 churches and chapels are left and in the past Goslar was famous for its silhouette rich in towers and belfries. The mediaeval market place is surrounded by many historical buildings. The old town hall faces the building with the Glockenspiel which commemorates the discovery, in the 10th Century, of the nearby silver mines which gave Goslar its wealth and prestige. Along the other side of the square is Kaiserworth, now a hotel which was originally the headquarters of the clothmakers' guild. The present building dates back to 1494.

A walk through the winding old streets of Goslar is a worthwhile experience. Picturesque old houses lean against each other as if they are looking for some support in their old age.

The forests of the surrounding Harz mountains offer beautiful views and relaxing walks. There are streams for swimming and boating and in winter the gentle slopes provide some good skiing.

Grüner Aal mit Gurkensalat

Eel with Cucumber Salad

Serves 4

1-1.5 kg (2-3 lb) fresh eel, cut into 5 cm
  (2 in) pieces
6 sprigs parsley
12 peppercorns
2 bay leaves
salt
juice ½ lemon

2 tablespoons butter
2 tablespoons flour
1 tablespoon chopped parsley
1 tablespoon chopped dill
1 teaspoon chopped chervil
½ cup (4 fl oz) sour cream

1. Place the eel, parsley, peppercorns, bay leaves, salt and lemon juice in a saucepan. Cover with water and simmer for 15 to 20 minutes.
2. Remove the eel and keep warm.
3. Reduce the cooking stock to 1 cup and strain.
4. Prepare a roux by melting the butter and stirring the flour into it. Without browning it, cook the roux for 5 minutes and then gradually add the hot and strained stock. Cook until it thickens into a smooth light sauce.
5. Add the parsley, dill and chervil together with the sour cream. Once the cream has been added do not cook it further.
6. Serve the eel pieces arranged on a serving platter with the sauce poured over them. Traditionally this dish is served with cucumber salad (see p. 12) and boiled potatoes.

Aal mit frischen Kräutern gebraten

Fried Eel with Herbs

From the Waldschlösschen Bösehof in Bederkase.

Serves 4

1 kg (2 lb) eel, cut into 10 cm (4 in) pieces
salt
freshly ground black pepper
½ cup (2 oz) flour
90 g (3 oz) butter

½ cup chopped fresh herbs (oregano,
  thyme, tarragon, etc.)
1 clove garlic, finely chopped
2 tomatoes, peeled and diced
6 champignon-type mushrooms, diced

1. Season the eel and dust with the flour.
2. In a frying pan, melt the butter and fry the eel. Add the herbs, garlic, tomatoes and mushrooms and cook for a further 5 minutes.
3. Traditionally the eel is served with parsley potatoes and a lettuce salad.

Hummer Ragout

Hamburg Lobster Ragout

Serves 4

1½ cups (12 fl oz) fish stock (see p. 137)
½ cup (4 fl oz) dry white wine
4 sprigs parsley
1 small onion, chopped 1 celery leaf, chopped
1 lamb or calf sweetbread
2 teaspoons lemon juice
2 tablespoons butter
2 tablespoons flour
1 can (approximately 200 g (6½ oz)) asparagus tips, drained

125 g (4 oz) button mushrooms
1 tablespoon capers
2 tablespoons sour cream
1 tablespoon chopped dill
500 g (1 lb) lobster meat, cooked and diced
2 egg yolks
4 slices toast

1. Combine the fish stock, wine, parsley, onion and celery leaf. Cook for 15 to 20 minutes. Strain and bring to the boil again. Add the sweetbread and lemon juice and simmer for 10 minutes. Remove the sweetbread and save the stock.
2. When the sweetbread is cool, remove the membranes and cut into small dice.
3. To prepare the sauce, melt the butter, add the flour and cook it, without browning, for 5 to 10 minutes. Heat the stock and slowly add it to the roux. Cook until the sauce is smooth and thick.
4. Add the asparagus, mushrooms and capers and cook for 5 minutes. Add the sour cream, dill, lobster meat and sweetbreads.
5. Beat the egg yolks and add some of the hot sauce to them. Pour the egg yolk mixture back into the sauce and simmer for 2 to 3 minutes until the sauce is smooth and creamy. Make sure the sauce does not cook too rapidly or it will curdle.
6. Serve the lobster and the sauce poured over the toast.

Kaiser Krabben mit Dillsosse

King Prawns in Dill Sauce

Serves 4

2 celery sprigs, chopped
1 onion, chopped
750 g (1½ lb) fresh prawns (shrimps) in their shells
45 g (1½ oz) butter

1 tablespoon flour
1 tablespoon finely chopped fresh dill
½ cup (4 fl oz) sour cream
salt
freshly ground black pepper

1. Cook the celery and onions in a little salted water for 10 minutes.
2. Add the prawns and cook until they turn pink (approximately 2 to 3 minutes).
3. Cool the prawns in the stock. Remove and shell them, strain and reserve the stock.
4. To make the sauce, melt the butter in a saucepan, stir in the flour and cook for a few minutes without browning.
5. Add the dill and 1 cup of the prawn stock.
6. Cook for a few minutes until the sauce thickens. Finally add the sour cream and the prawns. Season before serving.

Poultry

For centuries the roast goose of Germany was considered to be the most festive of all dishes. Christmas and New Year's celebrations always featured that splendid bird. The tantalising smell of a freshly roasted goose with a chestnut, apple and marjoram filling is not easily forgotten and Germans often become quite nostalgic about it.

The goose makes a rich meal and changing dietary ideas have been responsible for its diminishing popularity.

The duck has always been well loved and is still going strong. Some of the best birds come from an area not far from Hamburg and the Vierländer Ente, stuffed with apple and ham takes its name after the district of its origin.

The turkey is not frequently prepared and there is a saying that "die Pute" (the turkey) is only as good as its stuffing and the side dishes that are served with it, such as salads or cranberries.

Today the chicken is more popular in Germany than it used to be in the past, consequently there are not many exciting traditional recipes. The Germans prefer their chickens simply roasted or fried in a crisp crust of breadcrumbs. The Bremer Kukenragout is well known and chicken, boiled with lots of fresh vegetables not only produces a deliciously tasting meat but the broth is eaten as a nourishing soup.

Despite the casual attitude of German cooks to chicken, one of the best chicken dishes I have ever eaten was in Bavaria where a spit-roasted Brathändl surpassed any I have had before or since.

Bremer Kükenragout
Chicken Ragout with Tongue, Brains and Prawns

Serves 6

125 g (4 oz) fresh tongue
1.5 kg (3 lb) chicken
1 tablespoon vinegar
1 calf's brain
60 g (2 oz) butter
250 g (8 oz) fresh mushrooms
1 tablespoon flour

2 egg yolks
1 cup (8 fl oz) cream
250 g (8 oz) prawns (shrimps), cooked,
  shelled, and chopped
125 g (4 oz) green peas, cooked
¼ cup finely chopped parsley

1. Cook the tongue in salted water for 1½ hours. Add the chicken and cook for a further hour.
2. When cooked, remove the chicken and tongue. Bone the chicken and dice the chicken meat and the tongue. Strain the cooking stock and reserve.
3. Add the vinegar to the stock and blanch the brain for about 10 minutes. Cool, remove the membranes and dice.
4. Sauté the mushrooms in 30 g of the butter until they are light brown. Remove the mushrooms.
5. To make a roux, add the flour to the butter in the pan and cook for 5 minutes. Add 1½ cups of the reserved stock to the roux and simmer for 10 minutes.
6. Beat the egg yolks until creamy, add ½ cup of hot chicken stock and add the egg mixture to the sauce. Add the remaining butter and beat over very low heat until the mixture thickens. Remove from the heat and add the cream.
7. Add the chicken, tongue and brain to the sauce together with the chopped prawns, mushrooms and peas. Taste, and if necessary, adjust the seasoning.
8. Serve the ragout sprinkled with chopped parsley. Traditionally this dish is eaten with freshly baked puff pastry crescents.

Berliner Hähnchen
Chicken Stuffed with Rice and Grapes

Serves 4

250 g (8 oz) cooked rice (use about 60 g
  (2 oz) uncooked rice)
1 onion, chopped
2 stalks celery, chopped
75 g (2½ oz) seedless grapes
½ cup (2 oz) slivered almonds, roasted

salt
freshly ground black pepper
½ tablespoon chopped fresh thyme
1.5 kg (3 lb) chicken
60 g (2 oz) butter, melted

1. Preheat the oven to 180°C (350°F/Gas 4).
2. In a mixing bowl, combine the rice, onion, celery, grapes, almonds, seasoning and thyme.
3. Place this stuffing in the chicken cavity and use a skewer to secure the opening.
4. Place the chicken in a roasting pan and pour over some of the melted butter. Season with salt and pepper. Roast the chicken for 1 to 1¼ hours until brown, basting occasionally with the melted butter.

Huhn mit Champignons
Chicken with Mushrooms

Serves 4

1.5 kg (3 lb) chicken, cut into pieces
45 g (1½ oz) butter
juice of 1 lemon
3 sprigs parsley, chopped
375 g (12 oz) mushrooms, sliced

100 g (3½ oz) meaty Speck or smoked
    bacon cut into strips
1 tablespoon tomato paste
2 cups (16 fl oz) dry white wine
salt
freshly ground black pepper

1. Preheat oven to 180°C (350°F/Gas 4).
2. In a frying pan, brown the chicken pieces in the butter then sprinkle with the lemon juice.
3. Add the parsley, mushrooms, Speck or bacon.
4. Dilute the tomato paste in the wine and add to the mushrooms. Season.
5. Transfer to a roasting dish, place in the preheated oven and cook, uncovered, for 45 minutes turning occasionally until the chicken is cooked.

Berliner Hühner-Frikassé
Chicken Fricassee

Serves 4-6

1.5 kg (3 lb) chicken, cut into pieces
salt
freshly ground black pepper
45 g (1½ oz) butter
30 g (1 oz) flour
2 cups (16 fl oz) hot chicken stock
   (see p. 134) or water

½ cup (4 fl oz) dry white wine
375 g (12 oz) button mushrooms, sliced
250 g (8 oz) fresh asparagus, peeled and
    cut into 2.5 cm (1 in) pieces
½ cup (4 fl oz) cream
juice of 1 lemon
4 sprigs parsley, finely chopped

1. Sprinkle the chicken pieces with pepper and salt and fry them in the butter until brown on all sides.
2. Sprinkle with flour and cook for 2-3 minutes over low heat.
3. Add the chicken stock and wine and cook for 5 minutes.
4. Add mushrooms and asparagus, cover and simmer on low heat for 45 minutes.
5. Add cream, lemon juice, adjust the seasoning and serve hot with boiled rice and sprinkled with parsley.

Hühner Soufflé
Chicken Soufflé

Serves 4-6

½ onion, finely chopped
60 g (2 oz) butter
3 tablespoons flour
2 cups (16 fl oz) hot milk
salt
freshly ground black pepper
60 g (2 oz) dry breadcrumbs

1 cup (4 oz) grated Gruyére-style
   cheese
250 g (8 oz) chicken meat, finely
   chopped
4 eggs, separated
3 sprigs parsley, finely chopped

1. Preheat the oven to 180°C (350°F/Gas 4).
2. Lightly fry the onions in the butter, add the flour, cook for 3 minutes and add the hot milk, stirring constantly.
3. Add the breadcrumbs, stir and cook until smooth. Season.
4. Remove from the heat and mix in the grated cheese, chicken meat and egg yolks.
5. Beat the egg whites until they hold stiff peaks.
6. Gently fold them into the chicken mixture. Add the parsley.
7. Pour the mixture into a buttered soufflé dish and bake in the preheated oven for 35-40 minutes. Serve hot with a green salad.

Backhähnchen nach Süddeutscher Art

Ginger Crumbed Fried Chicken

Serves 6

1.5 kg (3 lb) chicken	**¼ teaspoon powdered ginger**
salt	**60 g (2 oz) butter**
2 eggs, whipped	**3 tablespoons olive oil**
1 cup (4 oz) dry breadcrumbs	**6 lemon wedges**
½ cup (2 oz) grated Parmesan cheese	

1. Preheat the oven to 200°C (400°F/Gas 6).
2. Cut the chicken into serving-sized pieces, rub them with salt, dip them in the egg, and roll them in a mixture of breadcrumbs, cheese and ginger.
3. Heat the oil and butter in a frying pan and brown the chicken on all sides.
4. Transfer the chicken to a roasting tray and bake for 20 to 30 minutes in the oven.
5. Serve the chicken pieces arranged on a platter, garnished with the lemon wedges.

Lübeck

Lübeck today is like Phoenix risen from the ashes. Badly damaged during the last war it has been lovingly restored.

In the Middle Ages it was a member of the powerful Hanseatic League and was known as the "Queen of the Hanse". A title bestowed upon the city not only because of its power, wealth and influence, but also because of its attractive appearance. The narrow, winding streets were flanked by proud, solid brick buildings, the residences and warehouses of the wealthy merchants.

Tall churches, impressive public buildings and impenetrable fortifications reflected the power and prosperity of its citizens.

One of the most attractive aspects of its appearance is the uniformity of colour and texture given off by the brick Gothic style so typical of the mediaeval architecture of northern Europe.

Huhn in Wein
Stewed Chicken in Wine

Serves 4

1.5 kg (3 lb) chicken
salt
freshly ground black pepper
45 g (1½ oz) butter
2 tablespoons finely chopped mixed
  herbs (such as rosemary, thyme or
  marjoram)

2 onions, chopped
½ cup (4 fl oz) chicken stock (see p. 134)
1 cup (8 fl oz) white wine
105 g (3½ oz) button mushrooms, sliced
½ tablespoon flour

1. Preheat the oven to 180°C (350°F/Gas 4).
2. Cut the chicken into pieces, season with salt and pepper, and fry in the butter until golden-brown.
3. Add the herbs and onions and continue frying until the onions are light brown.
4. Transfer to a cast-iron casserole. Add the chicken stock and wine and cover the pan.
5. Place the casserole in the oven for 45 minutes.
6. Add the mushrooms and return the casserole to the oven for a further 15 minutes.
7. When the chicken is cooked, blend the cooking juices with the flour. Taste and season if necessary.

Gebratene Hühnerleber
Fried Chicken Livers

Serves 4

90 g (3 oz) Speck or smoked bacon
1 onion, finely chopped
1 large cooking apple, peeled, cored
  and diced
200 g (6½ oz) chicken livers, roughly
  chopped
2 tablespoons flour

½ cup (4 fl oz) chicken stock (see p. 134)
  or water
½ cup (4 fl oz) dry white wine
juice of ½ lemon
3 sprigs parsley, finely chopped
salt
freshly ground black pepper

1. Fry the Speck or bacon, add the onion and apple and sauté for 3-5 minutes.
2. Add the livers and flour and cook for a further 3 minutes.
3. Pour in the stock, wine and lemon juice and simmer for 5 minutes.
4. Add parsley, season and serve hot with toasted bread.

Pommersches Entenklein
Pommeranian Giblet Stew

Serves 4-6

1 kg (2 lb) duck or chicken giblets
2 carrots, chopped
4 celery stalks, chopped
2 cloves
12 peppercorns

6 cups (1.5 litres) water
250 g (8 oz) mixed dried fruit, soaked
  overnight in water
2 tablespoons sugar
1 tablespoon white wine vinegar

1. Combine the giblets, carrots, celery, cloves and peppercorns. Add the water and cook for 1 hour. Remove the cloves and peppercorns.
2. Add the dried fruit, sugar and vinegar, season to taste and serve with mashed potatoes.

Lübecker Ente
Duckling Stuffed with Apples and Raisins

Serves 4

¾ cup (4 oz) raisins
1 cup (8 fl oz) white wine
500 g (1 lb) apples, peeled, cored and
  chopped into small dice
500 g (1 lb) white bread, cut into cubes

1 cup (8 fl oz) brandy
pinch cinnamon
freshly ground black pepper
salt
1.5 kg (3 lb) duckling

1. Preheat the oven to 180°C (350°F/Gas 4).
2. Soak the raisins in the wine for 30 minutes.
3. Combine the raisins and wine with the apples in a saucepan, add the bread and soak for 10 minutes.
4. Pour the brandy into the saucepan and flame.
5. Add the cinnamon and season with pepper and salt. If the mixture is too liquid, cook until some of the liquid evaporates.
6. Fill the duck with the stuffing, place it in a baking dish and roast for 1½ hours.
7. Serve with the cooking juices poured over.

Ente mit Sauerkraut auf Nürnberger Art

Duck with Sauerkraut, Apples and Grapes

Serves 4

2-2.5 kg (4-5 lb) duckling
juice 1 lemon
salt
freshly ground black pepper
1 onion, peeled

1 kg (2 lb) Sauerkraut
2 cooking apples, peeled and diced
2 cups (16 fl oz) dry white wine
60 g (2 oz) seedless grapes
2 tablespoons flour

1. Preheat the oven to 180°C (350°F/Gas 4).
2. Rub the skin of the duckling with lemon juice and sprinkle with salt and pepper.
3. Place the onion in the cavity and arrange the duck on a rack in a baking dish.
4. Place in the oven and roast for 1 hour. Drain off the excess fat from the pan while the duck is roasting.
5. Mix the Sauerkraut, apples and half a cup of the wine together, and simmer for 30 minutes.
6. Arrange the Sauerkraut in a casserole and half an hour before the duck is ready, remove it from the oven and place it on top of the Sauerkraut mixture. Sprinkle with the grapes, cover, and return to the oven to bake for a further 30 minutes.
7. In the meantime, remove as much of the fat as possible from the cooking juices. Mix a little of it with the flour to make a smooth paste and then stir this into the remainder. Add the remaining wine, season to taste and simmer for 15 minutes.
8. When the duck is cooked, carve it and arrange on a platter.
9. Add half the gravy to the Sauerkraut and serve the rest in a sauce-boat. Traditionally, the dish is served with mashed potatoes.

Opposite top: A selection of dishes from the Schabbelhaus. Clockwise from bottom left: Duckling Stuffed with Apples and Raisins (see p. 73); Red Fruit Dessert (see p. 113); Crayfish Soup (see p. 36).
Bottom: Four courses from the Parkhotel Fürstenhof. Clockwise from bottom left: The Duke's Duck Dinner; Heath Honey Parfait (see p. 121); Cucumber Soup (see p. 29); Prawns; Yoghurt Dressing (see p. 18).

Schabbelhaus, Lübeck

Since 1285, complete records have been kept of all the owners of merchants' houses at 48/50 Mengen Strasse in Lübeck.
Today the buildings are known as the Schabbelhaus and are the home of one of Germany's best restaurants.
Its culinary reputation is built on its fine interpretations of French nouvelle cuisine, and on serving north German and local specialities.

Parkhotel Fürstenhof, Celle

The town of Celle is a 'museum' of sixteenth and seventeenth century half-timbered architecture.
The Fürstenhof is in keeping with the calm, elegant feeling of Celle. Originally the seventeenth century home of a nobleman, the hotel is an example of quality and good taste.
The dining room is an excellent setting for the fine food it serves. It is called the Entenfang, after the duck-shooting pond which belonged to the local duke. Needless to say, duck is the speciality of the house and mine was number 5,461, prepared according to the princely old recipe.

Vierländer Ente
Duck with Apple and Ham Stuffing

Serves 4

2 kg (4 lb) duck
3 cooking apples, peeled and chopped
75 g (2½ oz) lean ham, diced
1 spring onion (scallion), chopped
60 g (2 oz) butter
¼ cup (½ oz) soft breadcrumbs

salt
freshly ground black pepper
juice 1 lemon
1 cup (8 fl oz) chicken stock (see p. 134)
¼ cup (2 fl oz) sour cream

1. Preheat the oven to 180°C (350°F/Gas 4).
2. Prepare the duck by pricking the skin all over so that the fat will run out during the cooking.
3. Sauté the apples, ham and spring onion in the butter. Add the breadcrumbs, salt and pepper, and mix well.
4. Stuff the breast cavity of the duck with this mixture.
5. Brush the outside of the duck with lemon juice mixed with salt and pepper.
6. Arrange the duck on a rack and roast it for 1½ hours. *Baste occasionally with chicken stock.*
7. When the duck is tender, remove it from the oven and pour off the pan juices. Skim off the fat from the pan juices, add the remaining chicken stock and sour cream and heat gently without boiling. Season and serve as a sauce poured over the duck.

Geschmorte Ente mit Rüben
Braised Duckling with Turnips

Serves 4

2 kg (4 lb) duckling
75 g (2½ oz) butter
salt
freshly ground black pepper
30 g (1 oz) flour
1 cup (8 fl oz) hot chicken stock (see p. 134)

4 tablespoons tomato purée
1 cup (8 fl oz) dry red wine
4 turnips, diced
1 tablespoon sugar
1 tablespoon paprika
16 small pickling-type onions
½ cup (4 fl oz) sour cream

1. Preheat the oven to 180°C (350°F/Gas 4).
2. Fry the duckling in 45 g of the butter until it is brown on all sides. Season and transfer to a lidded casserole dish.
3. Add the flour to the butter in the pan and cook for 2 minutes.
4. Add the stock and stir until smooth and thick.
5. Add tomato purée and wine.
6. Pour this sauce over the duckling and braise in the oven for 40 minutes.
7. In the meantime brown the turnips in the remaining butter with the sugar.
8. Add the turnips, paprika and onions to the duckling, cover and continue cooking for a further 30 minutes.
9. Remove the duckling and carve it into portions. Add the sour cream to the sauce, adjust the seasoning, return the duck portions to the dish and serve hot directly from the casserole.

Gänsebraten

Pomeranian Roast Goose Stuffed with Prunes and Apples

Serves 6-8

4-5 kg (8-10 lb) goose
salt
freshly ground black pepper
2 onions, chopped
3-4 cups (24 fl oz-1 litre) water
2 cups (12 oz) pitted and chopped
   prunes

4 apples, peeled, cored and diced
1-1½ cups (2-3 oz) fresh, coarse, rye
   breadcrumbs
2 tablespoons sugar
75 g (2½ oz) flour

1. Twenty-four hours before roasting, rub the goose with the salt and pepper and refrigerate.
2. Place the goose in a large saucepan with the onions and water, and simmer, covered, for 1 hour.
3. Strain the stock, skim off the fat and reserve.
4. Rub the goose again with salt and pepper.
5. Preheat the oven to 220°C (425°F/Gas 7).
6. Combine the prunes, apples, breadcrumbs, sugar, salt and pepper and stuff the cavity of the bird. Use skewers to hold the opening together.
7. Place the goose breast side down on a rack in a roasting pan and bake for 45 minutes.
8. Drain the fat from the roasting pan, reduce the temperature to 190°C (375°F/Gas 5) and roast the goose for a further 1 to 1¼ hours.
9. Again, drain the fat from the pan. Turn the goose breast side up, and increase the temperature to 240°C (475°F/Gas 9). Roast for 15 minutes or until the breast is golden brown.
10. Remove the goose and keep warm.
11. Skim off the fat from the roasting pan but leave the cooking juices in it. Combine the flour with the reserved goose stock and add the mixture to the pan.
12. Slowly simmer until the sauce thickens. Season and serve it with the goose.

Game

Traditionally game was the food of noble lords who were the only ones privileged to hunt.

Today game is still something to be served on a special occasion even if it is just dinner in a favourite restaurant.

Game is seasonal and while modern refrigeration makes it available any time of the year, true connoisseurs like to eat it only during the hunting season. As with most meat, there is no substitute for the freshly killed, although some game, feathered as well as furred, requires hanging to tenderise its texture.

Game meat is usually lean and requires special care in its preparation. Venison, for example, must remain underdone if it is not to lose its delicate texture and flavour. It requires larding with fine strips of bacon fat, a treatment also given to the delicious meat of the hare.

Birds are either cooked in a casserole so that the moisture is preserved or roasted wrapped in very thin slices of Speck. The tiny quail as well as other small birds need very little cooking, especially when they are grilled.

It was customary to marinate game, especially venison and wild boar, and while the resulting flavours were strong and pleasant, the natural taste of the game was often lost. So today cooking methods which complement the meat are preferred. In Germany, sour cream is often used in sauces for venison and hare, while red wine and red currant jelly provide a piquant flavour. Herbs and especially juniper berries give the dishes an irresistible fragrance.

In season most quality restaurants serve a wide variety of game dishes which when washed down with fine German wines, are very much part of a long tradition of quality cooking.

Hirsch Kalbskeule 'Diana'

Venison 'Diana'

This receipe comes from the Hotelschloss in Spangenberg. The Hotelschloss is one of the many medieval German castles which have been converted into hotels and restaurants. In addition to the comfortable residential rooms, many of the original halls now serve as conference rooms. One, the old Knight's Hall, accommodates 300 people. The surrounding countryside supplies many of the ingredients for the kitchen: trout from local streams is prepared in a variety of ways and the freshwater crayfish is served in a delicate dill sauce. Game is popular and many traditional game recipes appear on the menu.

Serves 4

1 kg (2 lb) venison	**1 leek (white part only), chopped**
4-6 cups (1-1.5 litres) dry red wine	**3 stalks celery, chopped**
12 peppercorns	**3 onions, chopped**
4 bay leaves	**6 peppercorns, crushed**
12 juniper berries, crushed	**½ cup (4 fl oz) cream**
60 g (2 oz) butter	**250 g (8 oz) button mushrooms, sliced**
1 carrot, chopped	**and lightly sautéed in butter.**

1. Marinate the venison for 24 hours in a mixture of the red wine, peppercorns, bay leaves and juniper berries.
2. Preheat the oven to 180°C (350°F/Gas 4).
3. Remove the venison from the marinade and dry the meat. Reserve the marinade.
4. In a heavy-bottomed casserole, brown the meat in half the butter. Add the carrot, leek, celery, two-thirds of the onions and the marinade (solids and liquid).
5. Place the casserole in the oven and roast for 30 minutes, basting occasionally.
6. Remove the meat and keep it warm.
7. In a frying pan, fry the rest of the onions in the remaining butter. Add the crushed peppercorns and pour in the cooking liquid. Bring it to the boil.
8. Strain the liquid through a sieve and finally add the cream.
9. Cut the meat into slices, garnish it with the sliced mushrooms and mask it with the sauce.
10. The meat is traditionally served with stewed pears which have been filled with cranberry sauce.

Rehschnitzel gedünstet in Rahmsosse

Venison Steaks Braised in Cream

Serves 4

4 venison steaks	**45 g (1½ oz) butter**
30 g (1 oz) smoked Speck or bacon	**½ cup (4 fl oz) sour cream**
4 juniper berries, crushed	**½ cup (4 fl oz) beef stock (see p. 136)**
salt	**juice of ½ lemon**
freshly ground black pepper	**3 tablespoons dry red wine**
1-2 tablespoons flour	**125 g (4 oz) button mushrooms, sliced**

1. Tenderise the steaks with a meat hammer. Remove all membranes and make a few incisions around the edges so that they do not curl up during cooking.
2. Cut the Speck or bacon into small pieces with a sharp knife. Make incisions in the steaks and lard them with Speck or bacon.
3. Mix the juniper berries with salt and pepper, then rub it into both sides of the steaks, Dust them with the flour.
4. In a heavy-bottomed frying pan melt the butter and lightly brown the steaks on both sides.
5. Add the sour cream, stock, lemon juice, wine, mushrooms, salt and pepper.
6. Cover and braise over low heat for 20 minutes.
7. Serve with Spätzle (see p. 140) and braised red cabbage.

Gebratenes Rehschnitzel
Fried Venison Steaks

Serves 4

4 venison steaks
2-3 tablespoons wine vinegar
2 tablespoons olive oil
juice of 1 lemon
freshly ground black pepper
6 juniper berries, crushed
2 tablespoons red wine

45 g (1½ oz) butter
2 tablespoons brandy or cognac
salt
½ cup (4 fl oz) sour cream
4 tablespoons beef stock (see p. 136)
2-4 tablespoons dry red wine

1. Tenderise the steaks with a meat hammer. Remove all membranes and make a few incisions around the edges so that they do not curl up during cooking.
2. Make a marinade by combining the vinegar, oil, lemon juice, pepper, juniper berries and red wine.
3. Place the steaks in a glass or china dish and pour over the marinade. Refrigerate overnight.
4. Melt the butter in a heavy-bottomed frying pan. Fry the steaks for 3-5 minutes or until they are brown on the outside but still pink inside. Pour on the brandy, set it alight, and flambé until the flame dies down. Season.
5. Remove the steaks from pan. Set them aside and keep them warm.
6. Add the sour cream, stock and wine to the pan and cook for about 5 minutes. Season and pour over the steaks.
7. This dish is traditionally served with breadroll dumplings and braised red cabbage.

Schwarzwälder Rehpfeffer
Venison Pepper Stew

This recipe comes from the Burghotel in Sababurg.

Serves 4-6

1 kg (2 lb) venison (neck, shoulder or breast meat) cut into cubes
2 cups (16 fl oz) dry red wine
3 bay leaves
8 juniper berries, crushed
½ teaspoon dried thyme
1 onion studded with 6 cloves
6 peppercorns
2 slivers of lemon peel

125 g (4 oz) Speck or bacon, diced
salt
freshly ground black pepper
2 cups (16 fl oz) beef stock (see p. 136)
½ cup (4 fl oz) sour cream
3 tablespoons red currant jelly, heated to liquefy white pepper
white pepper
½ teaspoon grated lemon rind

1. Place the meat in a marinade of wine, bay leaves, juniper berries, thyme, onion and cloves, peppercorns and lemon peel. Refrigerate for 24 hours.
2. Drain the meat and reserve the marinade.
3. Lightly sauté the Speck or bacon to render the fat.
4. Add the venison to the pan and fry until brown. Season and add 1 cup of the stock. Cover and simmer over low heat for 50 minutes or until the meat is tender.
5. During that time gradually add the rest of the stock and all the strained marinade.
6. Add the sour cream, red currant jelly, sufficient white pepper to make the stew quite peppery, and the lemon rind.
7. Continue cooking gently for a further 5 minutes. Season to taste.
8. Serve with Spätzle (see p. 140), stewed apples and cranberries.

Gefüllter Fasan
Stuffed Pheasant

Serves 4-6

STUFFING
3 slices fresh white bread
30 g (1 oz) butter
heart, liver and giblets of the pheasant
125 g (4 oz) chicken livers
1 tablespoon chopped parsley
4 juniper berries, crushed
4 black peppercorns, crushed
pinch ground allspice
pinch dried thyme
pinch dried marjoram

PHEASANT
45 g (1½ oz) butter
juice of 1 lemon
1 teaspoon salt
1.5-2 kg (3-4 lb) pheasant
4 slices bacon
1 cup (8 fl oz) chicken stock (see p. 134)
pinch ground allspice
pinch dried thyme
pinch dried marjoram
½ cup (4 fl oz) sour cream

Stuffing
1. Cut the bread into small cubes and toast them in the oven for 10 minutes until they are brown all over. Set aside in a bowl.
2. In a frying pan, melt the butter and fry the heart, liver, giblets and chicken livers for 3 or 4 minutes.
3. Remove from the pan, chop and add to the toasted bread.
4. Scrape the remaining fat from the pan into the bread mixture, then add the parsley, juniper berries, peppercorns, allspice, thyme and marjoram. Mix well.

Pheasant
1. Preheat the oven to 180°C (350°F/Gas 4).
2. Combine the butter, lemon juice and salt, and rub the pheasant inside and out with it.
3. Loosely fill the cavity with the stuffing and close the opening with skewers. Cover the pheasant with the bacon.
4. Place the pheasant, breast side up in a baking dish and roast for 30 minutes.
5. Increase the oven temperature to 200°C (400°F/Gas 6). Remove and discard the bacon. Baste the pheasant with a little of the chicken stock, to which allspice, thyme and marjoram have been added, and roast for a further 30 minutes. Baste from time to time.
6. Test the pheasant by piercing the thigh with a knife. The juice should be clear and yellow. If it is pink, roast for a further 5 to 10 minutes.
7. Transfer the pheasant to a serving dish.
8. Make a sauce by pouring the remaining chicken stock into the pan and bringing it to the boil. Scrape all the bits clinging to the bottom and sides of the pan into the stock. Stir in the sour cream and simmer just to heat. Adjust the seasoning if necessary. Serve the sauce separately in a sauce-boat.

Burg Hornberg

The castle of Hornberg is a fine example of the many German castles, palaces, and manor houses which today serve as comfortable, up-to-date hotels and inns.

Burg is not far from Heidelberg along the B27 Neckartal Burgenstrasse. Since 1612 until the present, it has been in the possession of the von Gemmingen family. It was built in the 11th Century and it has a museum and art collection on show. Its prime claim to fame is that it was the residence of the famous 16th Century knight Götz von Berlichingen who, for his part in the peasant rising at the time, was prisoner for 16 years in his own house. Burg Hornberg offers fine wines from its own vineyards which are superb with the house speciality: spit-roasted meat.

Fasan geschmort mit Pilzen
Braised Pheasant with Mushrooms

Serves

1 pheasant, dressed
juice of 1 lemon
salt
freshly ground black pepper
45 g (1½ oz) butter
4 thin slices bacon
1 small onion, finely chopped

½ cup (4 fl oz) Madeira or sweet sherry
1 cup (8 fl oz) beef stock (see p. 136)
250 g (8 oz) button mushrooms,
 finely sliced
4 tablespoons cream
1 teaspoon flour

1. Paint the pheasant with half the lemon juice and sprinkle with salt and pepper. Melt the butter in a heavy lidded casserole and brown the pheasant.
2. Wrap the bird in the bacon and secure the bacon with string.
3. Sprinkle the outside with the rest of the lemon juice and brown the bacon on all sides.
4. Add the onion, half the Madeira or sherry and the stock. Cover and braise over low heat. Gradually add the rest of the Madeira.
5. Total braising time, depending upon the age of the bird is between 45 minutes and 1½ hours.
6. Twenty minutes before the bird is ready, add the mushrooms.
7. Mix the cream with the flour and add it to the cooking juices. Cook gently for another 5 minutes and season.
8. Remove the bacon, carve the bird and return the pieces to the casserole with the sauce and mushrooms. Serve it from the dish with dill potatoes.

Fasan mit Sauerkraut
Pheasant with Sauerkraut

Serves 4

1 pheasant
salt
freshly ground black pepper
3 slices bacon
3 onions, chopped
90 g (3 oz) butter

1 kg (2 lb) fresh Sauerkraut
2 cups (16 fl oz) chicken stock
 (see p. 134)
1 cup (8 fl oz) dry white wine
2 tablespoons brandy

1. Preheat the oven to 200°C (400°F/Gas 6).
2. Rub the pheasant inside and out with the salt and pepper.
3. Wrap the bacon around the bird, place it in a shallow oven dish and bake it for 20 minutes.
4. Sauté the onions in the butter.
5. Add the Sauerkraut to the onions. Cover and simmer for 15 minutes.
6. Remove the bird from the baking dish. Add the chicken stock and white wine to the pan juices. Cook until the liquid has reduced by half.
7. Add the Sauerkraut to the reduced cooking juices and mix well.
8. Place the pheasant on top of the Sauerkraut, using some of it to cover the bird lightly.
9. Return the pheasant to the oven, reduce the heat to 180°C (350°F/Gas 4) and cook for 1 more hour.
10. Arrange the Sauerkraut on a serving plate and place the bird on top of it. Pour the cooking juices over the pheasant. Warm the brandy, pour it over the bird, ignite it and serve it flaming.

Gebratene Rebhühner

Roast Partridge

Serves 4

4 young and tender partridges, dressed
salt
freshly ground black pepper
4 sprigs parsley, finely chopped
4 cooking apples, peeled, cored and
   roughly chopped
8 thin slices of bacon
45 g (1½ oz) butter

4 fresh basil leaves, chopped
1 onion, cut into quarters
6 juniper berries
heart and liver of the partridges,
   finely chopped
1 cup (8 fl oz) dry red wine
4 tablespoons cream
1 teaspoon cornflour (cornstarch)

1. Preheat the oven to 180°C (350°F/Gas 4).
2. Rub the birds inside and out with salt and pepper.
3. Place the parsley and apples in to the cavity.
4. Cover the birds with the bacon slices and secure them in position with twine.
5. In a heavy lidded casserole melt the butter, add the basil, onion, juniper berries, heart, liver and the partridges and fry for 5 minutes.
6. Cover the dish and place it in the preheated oven, gradually adding the wine to baste the birds.
7. After approximately 20 minutes remove the bacon slices, increase the heat to 240°C (475°F/Gas 9) and return the casserole to the oven without the lid.
8. Turn the birds after 5 minutes and brown for a further 5 minutes. Remove from the oven.
9. Mix the cream with the cornflour, pour it over the birds and cook on top of the stove over medium heat for 5 minutes.
10. Remove the birds, scrape out the apple stuffing, set the birds aside and keep them warm.
11. Put the apple into the sauce and rub it through sieve. Season.
12. Serve one partridge per person, masked with the sauce and accompanied by Sauerkraut and mashed potatoes.

Hasenpfeffer
Braised Hare in Red Wine

The original recipe is designed for hare, but it is usually easier to obtain rabbit, so the quantities have been shown for both.

Serves 4

3 cups (24 fl oz) red wine
¼ cup (2 fl oz) red wine vinegar
1 onion, chopped
salt
freshly ground black pepper
4 whole cloves
6 juniper berries, crushed

6 bay leaves
1 baron (saddle and back legs) of hare
or
2 barons (saddles and back legs) of rabbit
½ cup (2 oz) flour
60 g (2 oz) margarine

1. Make a marinade by combining the wine, vinegar, onion, salt, pepper, cloves, juniper berries and bay leaves.
2. Joint the meat by cutting off the back legs and cutting the saddle into two.
3. Place the meat in the marinade and refrigerate for 24 hours.
4. Remove the meat, dry it and dust it with the flour.
5. In a heavy-bottomed saucepan, melt the margarine and fry the meat until brown.
6. Pour the marinade over the meat, cover the saucepan and simmer over low heat for approximately 1 hour, or until the meat is tender.
7. Remove the meat from the saucepan and keep it warm.
8. Strain the cooking juice and return it to the pan. Cook it until it reduces by approximately half. If the resulting sauce is not thick enough, it may be thickened with a little flour.
9. To serve, arrange the meat on a serving platter and pour the sauce over it.

Karlsbader Hasen-Ragout
Hare Stew

This delicious dish originated across the border in Bohemia but has been adopted in Germany. Rabbit may be used instead of hare.

Serves 4-6

1 kg (2 lb) hare or rabbit meat cut into cubes
60 g (2 oz) butter
1 large onion, chopped
2 cups (16 fl oz) beef stock (see p. 136)
2 tablespoons tomato purée
2 bay leaves

8 juniper berries, crushed
½ teaspoon crushed caraway seeds
½ teaspoon dried thyme
2 tablespoons paprika
salt
freshly ground black pepper
1 cup (8 fl oz) sour cream

1. In a heavy lidded casserole, lightly sauté the meat in the butter.
2. Add the onion and fry until it is soft and transparent.
3. Add the stock, tomato purée, bay leaves, juniper berries, caraway seeds, thyme, paprika, salt and pepper.
4. Cover and simmer over low heat for 50 minutes.
5. Add the cream, mix well and gently simmer for a further 5 minutes. If necessary adjust seasoning.
6. This is traditionally served with potato dumplings, lettuce salad, apple and cranberry compote.

*Opposite top: Smoked eel, the speciality of the Spieker restaurant.
Bottom: Some of the house specialities of Kaiserworth.
From left: Pear 'Dame Blanche'; Crown of the House (a platter of grilled meats, poached eggs, vegetables and Choron sauce); Consommé Kaiserworth (see p. 33).*

Spieker, Bad Zwischenahn

Uwe Woggon from the German Tourist Office in Frankfurt promised that our visit to the Spieker in Bad Zwischenahn would be a special occasion. He even came all the way from Frankfurt to join us.

The Spieker is an old Friesian farmhouse serving simple peasant fare. Its fame is based on its speciality: smoked eel. The eels there are small, tender and freshly smoked, and their aroma fills the room.

A pile of these eels, each with a price tag, is placed before the diners who then embark on the ritual of eating them. The skin is pulled off with an unzipping action; the eel is held at each end, and the juicy, tender flesh is chewed off the backbone. Then the waiter brings special round tin spoons which he fills with a local Schnaps. This is downed in one gulp, accompanied by an appropriate drinking rhyme and often, a beer chaser. The ritual is repeated until all the eels are eaten.

It was a great night and I am told that I had a very good time.

Kaiserworth, Goslar

Goslar is one of Germany's most historical towns. Founded in the tenth century, it was for some time the seat of the German Emperors, and it still prides itself on its many well-preserved, ancient buildings.

It is one of these, with some of its foundation walls dating back to the eleventh century, that houses the hotel and restaurant Kaiserworth. Situated in a prominent position in the town's market square, Kaiserworth is one of its show-pieces. In its well-appointed dining rooms and vaulted cellars, Herr Mühlenkamp serves some fine food. Most of it is of an international character, but there are some local game dishes, as well as trout from the fast-flowing streams of the Harz mountains.

Hasenrücken nach Försterin Art
Saddle of Hare

The whole baron of hare (the saddle and the hind legs) may be used, in which case one hare is sufficient. If only the saddle is used, two are necessary. This recipe comes from Heger's Parkhotel Flora in the Black Forest.

Serves 4

1 baron or 2 saddles of hare
2 slices Speck or bacon, cut into strips
salt
freshly ground black pepper
30 g (1 oz) butter
1 cup (8 fl oz) dry red wine

1 cup (8 fl oz) cream
½ cup (4 fl oz) demi-glace (see p. 137)
185 g (6 oz) fresh or preserved
   cherries, stoned
12 juniper berries, crushed

1. Preheat the oven to 180°C (350°F/Gas 4).
2. With a sharp knife, make incisions at regular intervals in the baron or saddle and insert the strips of Speck or bacon.
3. Season and place the hare in a cast-iron casserole or baking dish and roast it in the butter for 15 to 20 minutes, basting occasionally. Remove and keep warm.
4. Place the dish in which the hare was roasted on the stove, add the wine and reduce to half.
5. Reduce the heat and add the cream, demi-glace, cherries and juniper berries and simmer gently for 5 minutes. Season.
6. Carve the hare and arrange the slices on a serving platter. Pour some of the sauce over the hare and serve the remainder in a sauce-boat.
7. Traditionally the hare is served with cranberry sauce, sautéed mushrooms, chestnut purée and a salad in season.

Kaninchen mit Senfsosse

Rabbit with Mustard Sauce

Serves 4

4 thighs and 2 saddles of rabbit, each
   cut in half
1 clove garlic, crushed
3 tablespoons prepared German
   mustard
salt
freshly ground black pepper

45 g (1½ oz) butter
1 onion, chopped
1 carrot, chopped
2 stalks celery, chopped
1½ cups (12 fl oz) dry white wine
½ cup (4 fl oz) sour cream
1 teaspoon flour

1. Preheat oven to 190°C (375°F/Gas 5).
2. Rub the pieces with a mixture of the garlic, mustard, salt and pepper. Place the rabbit pieces in an oven-proof glass or china dish and cover and refrigerate overnight.
3. Remove the meat and scrape the mustard mixture back into the dish. Reserve the mixture.
4. Melt the butter in a heavy baking dish and sauté the rabbit pieces together with the onion, carrot and celery.
5. Add the wine to the reserved mustard mixture and place the dish in the preheated oven. Bake, turning the pieces frequently for 1-1½ hours depending upon the tenderness of the meat.
6. Mix the cream with the flour and add it to the cooking juices. Season if necessary. If a stronger flavour is desired add more mustard.
7. Serve hot with Spätzle (see p. 140) and braised red cabbage.

Schwäbische Kaninchenpastete

Swabian Rabbit Pâté

Serves 8

½ packet frozen puff pastry
1 fresh rabbit
1 onion, chopped
1 clove garlic, crushed
250 g (8 oz) whole button mushrooms
60 g (2 oz) butter

½ cup chopped parsley
1 tablespoon chopped fresh mixed
   herbs
½ cup (4 fl oz) dry white wine
1 egg, beaten lightly

1. Thaw the pastry.
2. Preheat the oven to 180°C (350°F/Gas 4).
3. Remove the rabbit meat from the bones and cut into large chunks. Process the meat in a food processor until fine in texture.
4. Lightly fry the onion, garlic and mushrooms in the butter. Add the parsley, herbs and wine, and cook for about 5 minutes.
5. Blend this mixture in a food processor until it is fine in texture.
7. Mix the meat in with the onion mixture and season.
8. Place the meat in a terrine and cover with the pastry. Brush the pastry with the egg.
9. Place the terrine in the oven and bake for approximately 1 hour.
10. Serve the pâté from the terrine.

Meats

Germans have always been great meat eaters. They love their pork roasts and Schnitzels, Sauerbraten and Kasseler Rippchen mit Sauerkraut, but most of all they love the Wurst. It would be hard to imagine a German butcher's shop without the colourful display of sausages. Small and large, thick and thin, white, brown, red, black or orange. All very appetising, exuding their delicious and tantalising smoky fragrance.

The Germans are without any doubt the world's greatest sausage eaters. It is therefore not surprising that there are some 250-300 different types of Wurst. Taking advantage of their prosperity, most Germans eat meat or meat products three times a day.

They like hearty breakfasts, with slices of sausage and cheese on crispy rolls with steaming Bohnenkaffee, the 'real' coffee.

For Mittagessen, the main meal of the day, it is the roast, mostly potroasted and well done, that they prefer.

Pork is the favourite meat of Germans and in addition to the Braten (roast) every part of the animal is eaten. Smoked pork in the form of Kassler Rippchen is very popular. There are also pork stews and pork cooking sausages (the Bratwurst).

After pork, Germans like veal and eat Schnitzel in numerous guises. They like their beef potroasted and well done. Sauerbraten is the most popular beef dish in Germany, with many regions having their own version. Deutsches Beefsteak is a hamburger and Beefsteak Tartar, is raw minced beef, mixed with raw egg yolk, chopped onions, capers and anchovies, a delicious and popular dish.

Germans are also fond of stews and their names indicate the place of their origin: Gaisburger Marsch, Berliner Eintopf, Pichelsteiner etc.

The Germans do great things with offal and every part of the animal is prepared in some delicious way adding another aspect to the already great wealth of German meat cooking.

Rheinischer Sauerbraten
Sauerbraten, Rhineland Style (marinated in red wine)

Sauerbraten is marinated for 2 to 3 days before it is cooked.

Serves 8

2 kg (4 lb) rump steak in one piece
¼ cup (1 oz) flour
90 g (3 oz) butter
2 carrots, sliced
2 onions, quartered
1 tablespoon concentrated tomato
  purée
75 g (2½ oz) ginger biscuits or
  gingerbread, crushed
2 tablespoons sugar
½ cup (4 fl oz) red wine
1 cup (5 oz) raisins
½ cup (2 oz) slivered almonds

salt
freshly ground black pepper
cranberry preserve for garnish
MARINADE
4 cups (1 litre) dry red wine
1 cup (8 fl oz) water
juice of 1 lemon
125 g (4 oz) onions, thinly sliced
6 peppercorns
2 bay leaves
1 teaspoon finely chopped thyme
2 cloves
¼ teaspoon nutmeg
5 sprigs parsley, chopped

1. Place the meat in a bowl. In a saucepan, combine all the ingredients for the marinade except the parsley, and bring to the boil. Pour over the meat and cool. Add the chopped parsley.
2. Refrigerate the marinated meat for 2 to 3 days, turning from time to time.
3. Remove the meat and strain the marinade. Wipe the meat dry, sprinkle it with flour, and in a saucepan sauté it in the butter until it is brown on all sides.
4. Add the carrots, onions, tomato purée and 1 cup of the strained marinade.
5. Cover the saucepan and simmer for 2½ to 3 hours or until the meat is tender.
6. Remove the meat.
7. Purée the sauce in a blender and strain it, then add the rest of the marinade, the ginger biscuits, sugar, wine and raisins.
8. Boil the mixture until it thickens. Add the almonds and cook for another 5 minutes. Taste, and if necessary, adjust the seasoning.
9. Carve the meat into slices, pour the sauce over it and serve it with the cranberry preserve. The dish should be accompanied by potato dumplings, Spätzle (see p. 140) or egg noodles.

Bayerischer Sauerbraten
Bavarian Style Sauerbraten (marinated in beer)

Serves 8-10

2 kg (4 lb) boned shoulder of beef
3 tablespoons flour
60 g (2 oz) butter
1 lemon, thinly sliced
sugar to taste
salt
½ cup (4 fl oz) sour cream

MARINADE
4 cups (1 litre) beer
2 cups (16 fl oz) water
1 lemon, quartered
2 bay leaves
1 onion, sliced
2 cloves
1 tomato, peeled and chopped
6 peppercorns

1. Place the meat into a bowl.
2. Combine all the ingredients for the marinade and pour it over the meat. Refrigerate for 2 to 3 days, turning the meat several times.
3. Remove the meat and strain the marinade.
4. Wipe the meat dry, dust it with flour, and in a saucepan brown it in butter on all sides.
5. Add 1 cup of strained marinade, lemon slices, sugar and salt.
6. Simmer the meat in a covered saucepan for 2½ to 3 hours or until tender.
7. Remove the meat. Purée and strain the cooking juice. Add the sour cream and reheat the sauce, but do not boil.
8. Serve the sauce poured over the sliced meat. Traditionally this dish is accompanied by potato dumplings and red cabbage.

Sauerbraten auf Norddeutsche Art

North German Sauerbraten (marinated in buttermilk and lemon juice)

Serves 8

2 kg (4 lb) boned rump or shoulder of
  beef, or shoulder of pork
4 cups (1 litre) buttermilk
juice 1 lemon
2 cups (16 fl oz) red wine
2 cups (16 fl oz) water
1 tablespoon salt
2 bay leaves

6 peppercorns
1 tablespoon vinegar
60 g (2 oz) butter
¼ cup (1 oz) flour
75 g (2½ oz) ginger biscuits or
  gingerbread, crushed
¼ cup (1 oz) raisins or currants
2 teaspoons sugar

1. Place the meat in a bowl and cover it with a mixture of the buttermilk and lemon juice. Refrigerate for 2 days turning occasionally.
2. Remove the meat from the bowl and wash off the buttermilk.
3. Place the meat in a saucepan, and add the red wine, water, salt, bay leaves, peppercorns and vinegar.
4. Cook covered for 2½ to 3 hours or until tender.
5. Remove the meat and strain the stock. There should be approximately 3 cups.
6. Melt the butter in a saucepan and stir in the flour. Cook until light brown. Add the stock and simmer for 10 minutes. Add the ginger biscuits and the raisins or currants, and cook until the sauce thickens. Add the sugar and adjust the seasoning.
7. Carve the meat into slices and serve it with the sauce poured over.

Deutsches Beefsteak und Falscher Hase

German Hamburgers and Meatloaf (Mock Hare)

This recipe may be used for making German hamburgers, or may be made into a meatloaf which locally is called mock hare.

Serves 4

1 cup (4 oz) stale white breadcrumbs
¼ cup (2 fl oz) milk
500 g (1 lb) beef, minced or a mixture of
  beef, veal and pork, minced
1 teaspoon salt

1 egg, lightly beaten
1 tablespoon chopped parsley
1 onion, chopped
125 g (4 oz) lard

1. Soak the breadcrumbs in the milk and when they are soft, squeeze them out thoroughly.
2. Combine all the remaining ingredients except the lard and mix them well.
3. The mixture may now be formed into individual hamburgers or a meatloaf.
4. Fry the hamburgers in the hot lard until they are brown on each side.
5. Bake the meatloaf on a greased baking dish in a preheated oven for 1 to 1¼ hours at 180°C (350°F/Gas 4).

Variations

Beefsteak á la Mayer, served with a fried egg on top of each hamburger.
Beefsteak with onions, served with onion rings which have been fried in butter.
Bremer beefsteak. Omit the bread and milk and use ½ cup of mashed potatoes plus 2 tablespoons of sour cream instead.
Another popular variation is made by using half a teaspoon each of basil and marjoram instead of the parsley.

Königsberger Klopse
Konigsberg Meatballs

Serves 6

1 cup (2 oz) fresh breadcrumbs	**CAPER SAUCE**
500 g (1 lb) lean beef, minced	2 tablespoons butter
250 g (8 oz) pork, minced	1 spring onion (scallion), chopped
2 spring onions (scallions), chopped	2 tablespoons flour
½ teaspoon grated lemon rind	½ cup (4 fl oz) white wine
juice ½ lemon	1 egg yolk
1 tablespoon juice from jar of capers	1 tablespoon capers
2 anchovy fillets, chopped	juice ½ lemon
1 teaspoon salt	salt
freshly ground black pepper	freshly ground pepper
2 eggs, beaten	
1 egg white, beaten	
3-4 cups (24 fl oz-1 litre) beef stock (see p. 136)	

1. Soak the breadcrumbs in water, then squeeze out and add to the minced beef and pork. Mix well together. Add the spring onions, lemon rind, lemon and caper juice, anchovies, salt and pepper. Combine all ingredients, then add the beaten eggs and egg white.
2. When the mixture is smooth, form it into 5 cm (2 in) meatballs.
3. Bring the stock to the boil and while it is boiling rapidly, add the meatballs, making sure not to add too many at one time. Cook them for approximately 15 minutes until they rise to the surface. Remove the meatballs with a slotted spoon and keep them warm. Strain the cooking juice and set it aside.

Caper Sauce

1. Melt the butter in a saucepan. Add the spring onion and cook until it is soft. Stir in the flour and cook for a few minutes. Add 2½ to 3 cups of the strained cooking juice.
2. Add the wine and simmer for a few minutes until the mixture is smooth and thick. Reduce the heat and add the egg yolk. Make sure that the sauce does not boil as it will curdle. Add the capers, lemon juice and season to taste. If the sauce is too thick, add more stock.
3. To serve, add the meatballs to the sauce and keep them warm until they are ready to be served. Traditionally, they are served with potatoes and a green bean salad.

Regensburg

In 1979 Regensburg celebrated its 1800th anniversary. As the Castra Regina it was an important outpost of the Roman Empire guarding its border along the Danube against the old German tribes to the north. Remains of ancient Roman walls are preserved and in many cases form part of today's buildings.

Regensburg has the distinction among the larger German towns of having preserved its mediaeval character. The Cathedral of St. Peter is one of the country's first examples of Gothic architecture.

The city is also famous for its sausages which originated in the Middle Ages. The traditional Regensburger Bratwurst, the rather thick, short, juicy sausage is renowned for its piquant flavour.

A visitor can sit in the open along the banks of the fast flowing Danube and enjoy this great local speciality washed down with fine Regensburg beer.

Pichelsteiner
Bavarian Picnic Stew

Serves 6

200 g (6½ oz) beef marrow
1 kg (2 lb) meat (beef, pork, lamb or a
    combination of the three), cut into
    large dice
1 small head of cabbage, chopped
500 g (1 lb) white turnips, peeled and
    diced
250 g (8 oz) green beans, cut into 2.5cm
    (1 in) lengths
1 celery root, sliced (if unavailable, use
    celery stalks)

2 potatoes, peeled and diced
1 large onion, chopped
2 tablespoons chopped parsley
salt
freshly ground black pepper
1 tablespoon paprika
2 tablespoons butter
2 cups (16 fl oz) beef stock (see p. 136)

1. Place the marrow bones in a saucepan, cover with water and bring them gently to the
   boil. Cook them for approximately 5 minutes and using a teaspoon, extract the marrow
   from the centre of the bone.
2. Place half the marrow in a heavy bottomed saucepan or casserole. Over this, place
   alternate layers of the meat and vegetables. Sprinkle each layer with salt, pepper and
   paprika. On top place the remaining marrow. Dot with butter and add the stock.
3. Cover the saucepan and simmer for 2 hours or until the meat is tender. Serve with
   dumplings.

Gaisburger Marsch
Beef Stew with Potatoes and Spätzle

Serves 6

500 g (1 lb) shin beef, cut into slivers
2 tablespoons lard
4 potatoes, peeled and cut into
    small dice
2 cups (16 fl oz) beef stock (see p. 136)
1 bay leaf

1 teaspoon vinegar
salt
freshly ground black pepper
1 recipe Spätzle (see p. 140)
2 large onions, sliced and fried
    separately in lard

1. In a saucepan, sauté the beef in lard until it is brown. Add the potatoes and cook for 5
   minutes, turning frequently.
2. Add the stock, bay leaf and vinegar. Reduce the heat and simmer for 30 minutes or until
   the meat and potatoes are tender. Season with salt and pepper.
3. Five minutes before the meat is cooked, add the Spätzle.
4. Serve the stew topped with fried onions.

Siebenbürgerfleish

Beef cooked in Milk from Siebenburgen

Serves 4

60 g (2 oz) Speck or smoked bacon,
   roughly chopped
1 kg (2 lb) beef rump or silverside
1 onion, roughly chopped
3 celery stalks, sliced
1 turnip, sliced
1 tablespoon dried basil
salt
freshly ground black pepper

3 cups (24 fl oz) milk
15 g (½ oz) butter
½ teaspoon sugar
2 tablespoons flour
1½ cups (12 fl oz) beef stock (see p. 136)
   or water
4 tablespoons sour cream
2 tablespoons tomato paste

1. Place the Speck or bacon in a heavy-bottomed, lidded casserole.
2. Add the meat, onion, celery, turnip, basil, salt, pepper and milk.
3. Cover, bring to the boil and gently simmer for 2 hours.
4. In the meantime, melt the butter, add the sugar and cook until it is light yellow. Add the flour and cook until it becomes golden yellow. Be very careful not to burn it, or it will taste bitter.
5. Add the stock or water and simmer for 10 minutes.
6. Pour this sauce over the meat for the last 10 minutes of cooking.
7. Mix the sour cream and tomato paste together and add it to the meat. Cook for 2 minutes more. If necessary adjust seasoning.
8. Remove the meat from the sauce, let it stand for 10 minutes and carve it into slices. Serve with the sauce and boiled potatoes or dumplings.

Sachsenhauser Topf

Beef, Pork and Veal Stew

Serves 6

500 g (1 lb) stewing beef, cut into
   large dice
250 g (8 oz) lean pork, cut into
   large dice
250 g (8 oz) stewing veal, cut into
   large dice
2 tablespoons flour
2 tablespoons lard
1 onion, chopped
1 clove garlic, crushed

1 tomato, peeled and chopped
3 potatoes, peeled and diced
3 cups (24 fl oz) water
3 cups (24 fl oz) dry white wine
2 tablespoons salt
250 g (8 oz) mushrooms, chopped and
   sautéed in butter
125 g (4 oz) fresh shelled peas
2 tablespoons chopped parsley

1. Sprinkle the meat with flour and fry it in the lard until browned on all sides. Transfer the meat to a large saucepan.
2. Add the onion and garlic to the lard and cook until light brown. Add the tomato and potatoes and continue frying for 1 minute. Add the water, wine and salt. Simmer for 2 to 3 minutes.
3. Pour the mixture over the meat, cover and simmer for 2½ to 3 hours.
4. Thirty minutes before cooking is completed, add the mushrooms and peas. Before serving, sprinkle the stew with parsley.

Weimarer Ochsenzunge

Beef Tongue with Raisin Sauce

Serves 6-8

1 fresh uncooked beef tongue
  (1.5-2 kg/3-4 lb)
1 onion, chopped
1 carrot, chopped
3 stalks celery, chopped
6 peppercorns
3 bay leaves
1 clove garlic, crushed

SAUCE
2 tablespoons butter
2 tablespoons flour
salt
2 tablespoons wine vinegar
3 tablespoons sour cream
1 teaspoon sugar
¾ cup (4 oz) raisins
freshly ground black pepper

1. Place the tongue in a large saucepan with the onion, carrot, celery, peppercorns, bay leaves and garlic. Cover with salted water and simmer for 2 hours.
2. Strain and reserve the stock and keep the tongue hot.
3. To make the sauce, melt the butter, add the flour and cook for 5 minutes.
4. Add 1½ cups (12 fl oz) of the reserved stock, the vinegar, sour cream, sugar and raisins. Cook together on a low heat for 3 minutes. Season.
5. Serve the tongue sliced with the raisin sauce.

Ochsenschwanz in dunkler Sosse

Oxtail Ragout

Serves 4

2 kg (4 lb) oxtail, cut into pieces
8 cups (2 litres) water
salt
2 onions, chopped
1 carrot, chopped
2 stalks celery, chopped
1 turnip, sliced
1 tablespoon dried marjoram
3 sprigs parsley, chopped

3 peppercorns
2 cloves
3 bay leaves
30 g (1 oz) lard
45 g (1½ oz) flour
2 tablespoons tomato purée
½ cup (4 fl oz) sour cream
1 cup (8 fl oz) dry red wine

1. Place the oxtail pieces in a large saucepan, add water, salt, onion, carrot, celery, turnip, marjoram, parsley, peppercorns, cloves and bay leaves.
2. Bring to the boil and simmer over low heat for 2-3 hours or until the meat is tender.
3. Remove the meat, strain the stock, skim off the fat and reserve the stock.
4. Take the meat off the bones and chop it into chunks.
5. Melt the lard, add the flour and cook until golden. Add the reserved stock and continue cooking for 5 minutes.
6. Add the tomato purée mixed with cream and the wine. Cook for 5 minutes.
7. Add the meat, season and serve hot with potato pancakes.

Opposite: Some of the simple Bavarian food served at Posthotel Koblerbräu.
From left: Liver Dumplings (see p. 30) and Smoked Pork Ribs with Sauerkraut; Apple Fritters (see p. 112).

Posthotel Koblerbräu, Bad Tölz

The Koblerbräu combines the best of two worlds. It has restored and maintained its old brewery and mail coach station, and added comfortable hotel facilities. The traditional Bavarian food is served in simple, pleasant surroundings. Typical dishes are smoked pork ribs with Sauerkraut, liver dumpling soup and local sausages. It is difficult to imagine a Bavarian meal without beer, and only the best is served at the Koblerbräu.

Fleischpudding
Meat Pudding

Serves 6-8

500 g (1 lb) lean pork meat, minced
250 g (8 oz) veal, minced
3 stale bread rolls, soaked in water for
   10 minutes and squeezed dry
1 onion, finely chopped
3 sprigs parsley, finely chopped
3 sprigs fresh herbs, chipped (such as
   thyme, marjoram or basil)

grated peel of ½ lemon
3 eggs, separated
salt
freshly ground black pepper
dry breadcrumbs

1. In a bowl thoroughly mix together the meat, bread rolls, onion, parsley, herbs, lemon peel and egg yolks. Season to taste.
2. Whip the egg whites until they are stiff and fold them into the mixture.
3. Grease a pudding mould, sprinkle it with breadcrumbs and fill it with the meat mixture.
4. Place the mould into a large saucepan and pour in enough water to come 5 cm (2 in) up the sides of the pudding mould.
5. Cover the saucepan, bring the water to the boil and simmer for 1½ hours.
6. Take the lid off the saucepan and let the pudding stand for 5 minutes. With a knife, carefully prise the meat from the sides of the mould and unmould it on to a serving platter.
7. Traditionally the meat pudding is served with a tomato, herb, caper or cheese sauce, boiled potatoes and a green salad.

Kasseler Rippchen
Cured Smoked Pork Ribs

Serves 4-6

1 kg (2 lb) cured smoked pork ribs
   (available at most delicatessen shops)
1 large onion, sliced
1 tomato, peeled and chopped
4 cups (1 litre) boiling water

2 tablespoons flour
1 tablespoon butter
salt
freshly ground black pepper
½ cup (4 fl oz) sour cream

1. Preheat the oven to 180°C (350°F/Gas 4).
2. In a baking dish, place the meat on top of the onion and tomato. Bake covered for 30 minutes.
3. Uncover, add 1 cup of boiling water and roast the meat for a further 1½ to 2 hours, adding the remainder of the water as it becomes necessary.
4. Remove the meat. Bring the liquid in the baking dish to the boil and scrape up all the caramelised bits of juice. Purée and strain the liquid.
5. Melt the butter in a pan, add the flour and stir over a moderate heat for 5 minutes. Slowly add the strained cooking juice and stir until the sauce is smooth. Adjust the seasoning if necessary. Remove from the heat and add the sour cream.
6. Carve the pork ribs into slices and pour the sauce over them. Traditionally, this dish is served with Sauerkraut and parsley potatoes.

Bratwurst in Bier, Berliner Art
Berlin Pork Sausages in Beer

Serves 6

12 Bratwurst (German pork sausages)
1 teaspoon butter
freshly ground black pepper

1 cup (8 fl oz) beer
2 teaspoons cornflour (cornstarch)
salt

1. In a saucepan, boil the sausages in water for 3 minutes. Drain.
2. Melt the butter in a frying pan and brown the sausages on all sides. Drain off the fat. Add the pepper and beer and simmer for 15 minutes. Thicken the sauce with cornflour first mixed to a paste with a little of the beer and add salt to taste.
3. The sausages are traditionally served with mashed potatoes.

Fränkischer Schmartelbraten
Roast Breast of Pork

Serves 4

1 kg (2 lb) lean breast of pork with skin
4 pork tails (optional)
1 clove garlic, crushed
salt
freshly ground black pepper

30 g (1 oz) lard
1 cup (8 fl oz) beer
1 cup (8 fl oz) beef stock (see p. 136)
2 onions, cut into quarters

1. Preheat the oven to 220°C (425°F/Gas 7).
2. With a sharp knife cut a criss-cross pattern into the skin of the meat.
3. Mix the garlic, salt and pepper together and smear it over the surface of the breast and tails.
4. In a heavy-bottomed pan fry the breast and tails in the lard until they are brown.
5. Place the meat in a baking dish and roast in the preheated oven for 45 minutes, basting frequently with a mixture of the beer and stock.
6. Add the onions, reduce the heat to 175°C (350°F/Gas 4) and cook for 45 minutes more.
7. Serve hot with the cooking juices, potato dumplings and braised cabbage.

Schlesisches Himmelreich
Casserole of Pickled Pork and Dried Fruit

Serves 4

500 g (1 lb) mixed dried apples, pears
   and pitted prunes
2 cups (16 fl oz) water
500 g (1 lb) pickled pork, diced
2 tablespoons butter

2 tablespoons cornflour (cornstarch)
¼ teaspoon powdered cloves
sugar
¼ teaspoon salt (optional)

1. Soak the dried fruit in the water for 3 to 4 hours.
2. Sauté the pork in the butter until it is light brown on all sides, then put it in a large saucepan.
3. Drain the dried fruit and reserve the liquid. Place the fruit around the meat.
4. Add the cornflour to the butter remaining in the pan and stir in the liquid from the fruit. Simmer for a few minutes until it thickens.
5. Add the cloves and the sugar to taste, and if necessary, a quarter of a teaspoon of salt. Pour the sauce over the meat and fruit.
6. Cover the saucepan and cook on a low flame on the top of the stove for 20 to 30 minutes. This dish is traditionally served with potato dumplings.

Labskaus
Sailor's Pork Hash

Serves 4

750 g (1½ lb) pickled pork
6 potatoes
1 large onion, chopped
90 g (3 oz) lard

3 pickled herring fillets, chopped
2 anchovy fillets, chopped
170 g (5½ oz) pickled beetroot, chopped
4 eggs

1. Cook the pickled pork in enough water to cover the meat for 2 hours or until tender.
2. Allow to cool, dice and put the pork through a food processor or meat grinder.
3. Boil the potatoes in their jackets in salted water. Drain, peel and mash.
4. Sauté the onion in the lard until golden-brown.
5. Remove the onions from the pan and mix them with the minced meat, potatoes, herrings, anchovies and beetroot.
6. Place the mixture back in the pan and cook, stirring it occasionally, until the hash has heated through.
7. Fry the eggs separately. Divide the hash into four and serve with a fried egg on top of each serving.

Hausmacher Sülze
Homemade Brawn

From the Brauereiausschank Schlenkerla in Bamberg. It is customary to have a beer 'bar' attached to a brewery, and while they originally served only beer, such places have often developed into restaurants. The Schlenkerla brewery has been making a special type of smoked-flavoured beer since 1678. Today the adjoining restaurant specialises in local peasant-type dishes: pig's trotters, veal knuckles, local sausages, brawns and pickled meats, all served with Sauerkraut and potato salad in the Bavarian tradition. Everthing they serve has a rich flavour and the aroma fills the ancient beamed and panelled rooms. The place is always packed with people who come from far and wide to enjoy the friendly atmosphere. Plenty of beer flows to wash down the highly flavoured fare.

Serves 6

½ pig's head	2 onions, cut into quarters
4 pig's trotters	3 cloves
6 tablespoons vinegar	1 tablespoon salt
8 juniper berries	3 tablespoons sugar
4 bay leaves	16 cups (4 litres) water
8 peppercorns	

1. Place all the ingredients in a large saucepan. and slowly bring them to the boil. Continue boiling for 1½ hours or until the meat is soft.
2. Remove the meat from the liquid and continue cooking until the liquid has reduced to approximately 6 cups.
3. Strain the solids out of the liquid and allow it to cool. Remove any fat.
4. Taste the liquid, and if necessary season or add more vinegar.
5. Remove the meat from the pig's head and the trotters and cut it into small cubes.
6. Place the meat into a decorative form or pâté mould and carefully pour the cold liquid over it.
7. Place it in a refrigerator and serve when it has set. Traditionally, fried potatoes and Schlenkerla smoked beer are served with the brawn.

Bernkastel an der Mosel

Every year the people of Bernkastel and the neighbouring villages celebrate the wine festival. Indeed there is good reason for rejoicing. The vineyards of the central Moselle district produce not only the finest Moselle wine, but together with the best from the Rhine, they yield white wines of the highest quality in Germany.

The highlight of the merriment is the crowning of the newly elected queen of the festival who arrives in grand style surrounded by her fair ladies-in-waiting.

In the market square the traditional proclamation is read, bands play oompah music and songs are sung in praise of the queen and the Moselle wine. Once the official celebrations are over, everyone adjourns to the 'Weinstrasse' along the river embankment where each of the wine villages from the district has its own stand offering its very best wines. It is a great treat as the wines sold are usually not obtainable anywhere else.

Stalls with spit-roasted meat, local sausages with Sauerkraut, potato pancakes, doughnuts and other delicious dishes are offered. Bernkastel, with its half-timbered houses, narrow winding streets, the surrounding hills covered with the steepest of vineyards, the castle and the tranquil river is the most attractive of romantic towns which nestle between the river and the vineyards.

Schweinefilet mit Biersosse

Pork fillet with Beer Sauce

Serves 4

750 g (1½ lb) pork fillets
150 g (5 oz) Speck or smoked
   bacon slices
2 spring onions (scallions), chopped
salt

freshly ground black pepper
1 cup (8 fl oz) cream
½ cup (4 fl oz) beer
600 g (1 lb 3½ oz) leeks, sliced
60 g (2 oz) butter

1. Preheat the oven to 200°C (400°F/Gas 6).
2. Trim the fat and sinews from the fillets and wrap the Speck or bacon around them, securing with tooth picks.
3. Heat a frying pan and brown the Speck-wrapped fillets on all sides.
4. Place the fillets in a baking dish and cook in the preheated oven for 15 minutes.
5. Remove the fillets and keep them warm.
6. Sauté the spring onions in the fat remaining in the baking dish. Add the cream and reduce by half. Add the beer and simmer. Season.
7. Remove the Speck from the fillets, finely chop it and set aside.
8. Lightly sauté the leeks in the butter and season them.
9. To serve, slice the fillet and arrange the slices on a bed of leeks, sprinkled with chopped Speck and masked with the sauce.

Eisbein gekocht mit Sauerkraut

Pickled Pork with Sauerkraut

Serves 4

30 g (1 oz) lard
2 onions, chopped
750 g (1½ lb) Sauerkraut
2 cooking apples, peeled, cored and
   roughly chopped
6 juniper berries, crushed

freshly ground black pepper
2 cloves
1 clove garlic, crushed
2 cups (16 fl oz) beef stock (see p. 136)
   or water
2 hands or knuckles of pickled pork

1. In a large lidded saucepan melt the lard and lightly fry the onions.
2. Add the Sauerkraut, apples, juniper berries, pepper, cloves, garlic and stock and cook for 10 minutes.
3. Make a well in the Sauerkraut, add the meat and cover with Sauerkraut.
4. Cover the saucepan and simmer over very low heat for 2 hours.
5. Remove the pork from the pan, take the meat off the bones and cut it into serving pieces.
6. If necessary, season the Sauerkraut, place it on a serving platter and arrange the meat on top of it. Serve with boiled potatoes or dumplings.

Gebratene Kalbsleber auf Berliner Art

Fried Calves' Liver with Apples and Onion, Berlin Style

Serves 4

125 g (4 oz) butter
2 onions, cut into thin slices and
    pushed into rings
750 g (1½ lb) cooking apples, peeled,
    cored and sliced

salt
freshly ground black pepper
500 g (1 lb) calves' liver, cut into 6 mm
    (¼ in) slices
flour

1. Melt half the butter in a frying pan. Fry the onion rings and apples slices until they are light brown. Season with salt and pepper. Set aside and keep hot.
2. Dust the liver slices with flour. Fry them in the remaining butter, allowing approximately 2 minutes each side. Do not overcook.
3. Serve the liver slices garnished with the apples and onions.

Kalbshaxe

Braised Veal Knuckle

Serves 4

4 small veal shanks
½ cup (2 oz) flour
2 tablespoons oil
2 tablespoons butter
2 onions, chopped
1 carrot, sliced
2 celery stalks, chopped

1 teaspoon paprika
¼ teaspoon thyme
¼ teaspoon basil
1 tablespoon chopped parsley
salt
freshly ground black pepper
2 cups (16 fl oz) beef stock (see p. 136)

1. Preheat the oven to 180°C (350°F/Gas 4).
2. Dust the veal shanks with flour and fry them in the oil and butter until they are brown. Remove and reserve.
3. In a heavy casserole, using the oil and butter mixture fry the onions, carrot and celery until they are light brown. Add the paprika, thyme, basil, parsley, salt and pepper. Place the shanks on top of the vegetables and pour in the beef stock.
4. Cover the casserole and cook in the oven for 2½ hours.
5. By the time the shanks are braised, the cooking juice should be thick like a sauce and should not require further thickening. Taste, and if necessary adjust the seasoning. Traditionally, the veal shanks are served with potato dumplings or noodles.

Kalbsbrägen
Crumbed Calves' Brains

Serves 4

4 calves' brains	1 cup (4 oz) fine dry breadcrumbs
juice of 1 lemon	60 g (2 oz) butter
salt	12 parsley sprigs
¼ cup (1 oz) flour	4 lemon slices
1 egg, beaten	

1. Place the brains under running water for 1 hour.
2. Half-fill a pan with water, bring to the boil, add the lemon juice and salt and blanch the brains for 10 minutes. Rinse them in cold water and allow to cool. Peel off the membranes.
3. Slice each brain into three.
4. Dip each slice in flour, then in the beaten egg, and finally coat each slice in breadcrumbs.
5. Heat the butter and fry the slices until they are crisp on each side. Remove the brain slices and keep them hot.
6. Add the parsley sprigs to the butter and fry until crisp. To serve, garnish the brain slices with the fried parsley and lemon slices. Serve with tartare sauce.

Kalbsherz mit Spinat und gebratenen Zwiebeln
Veal Heart with Spinach and Onions

From the Waldhotel Krautkrämer in Münster-Hiltrup. Hotel Krautkrämer is reputed to be one of the finest hotels in Germany, and its one-star Michelin Guide restaurant serves excellent food. My meal there was probably the best of my German tour. Great care is taken with food preparation, and the service in the dining room is excellent. Although most of the dishes on the menu have an international character, some of the venison and wild pig dishes are prepared according to local tradition. The saddle of venison in cream sauce is unforgettable. If requested, the chef will prepare local dishes, like broad beans with Speck and Mettenden (a local air-dried sausage), or veal heart with spinach, fried onions and parsley potatoes. Lamb dishes are also very popular here, while beer is the principal drink. It is even used to marinate fresh fruit, which is then served as a dessert.

The beautiful lakeside setting of the Krautkrämer, combined with its excellent cuisine, makes it a popular holiday resort.

Serves 6

1.25 kg (2½ lb) veal heart	600 g (1½ lb) spinach leaves
salt	1¼ cups (10 fl oz) cream
freshly ground black pepper	600 g (1¼ lb) onions, cut into sixths
2 tablespoons olive oil	60 g (2 oz) butter

1. Cut the veal heart into slices, each weighing approximately 200 g (6½ oz). Season them with salt and pepper and lightly fry them in oil for 3 to 5 minutes or until they are cooked but still pink inside.
2. Wash the spinach leaves thoroughly, blanch in water, and chop them.
3. Reduce the cream by approximately one-third and add the spinach. Keep it warm but do not cook it any further.
4. Fry the onions in the butter.
5. Arrange on each plate one or two slices of the veal heart and serve with the spinach in cream and fried onions.

Opposite: Allgauer Farmer's Plate and Liver Dumpling Soup from the Schlosshotel.

Schlosshotel, Hochenschwangau

Both of mad King Ludwig's castles, the Hochenschwangau and Niederschwanstein look down on the Schlosshotel.

Its beautiful setting is the starting point for excursions into one of Bavaria's most romantic areas. A visit to Niederschwanstein, that fairytale castle inspired by Wagner's operas of the Ring Cycle, is an experience of a lifetime.

Like most good German hotels, the Schloss offers a wide range of international dishes. However it also serves tasty local Bavarian dishes: The Allgäuer Farmers' Plate offers smoked pork ribs, pork sausages, Sauerkraut and bread roll dumplings, and Leberknödelsuppe, a clear consomme with liver dumplings is particularly tasty. The area also produces some very good cheeses and butter.

Kalbshaxe
Veal Knuckles

From the Goldene Sonne in Landshut.

Serves 4

2 medium-sized veal knuckles
45 g (1½ oz) lard, melted
salt
freshly ground black pepper
2 teaspoons paprika

2 onions, roughly chopped
2 tablespoons chopped
    mixed fresh herbs
2 cups (16 fl oz) beef stock (see p. 136)

1. Preheat the oven to 200°C (400°F/Gas 6).
2. Trim the veal knuckles, place them in a baking dish, and pour some of the melted lard over them. Season with salt, pepper and paprika and place the onions around them. Sprinkle the herbs over the knuckles. Add the beef stock.
3. Bake for 1½ to 2 hours, turning the knuckles frequently during cooking to allow them to brown evenly, and baste them with the beef stock.
4. Remove the knuckles from the oven and strain off the cooking juices through a sieve. If necessary, add more beef stock and season. Use these cooking juices as a gravy.
5. To serve, cut the meat off the bones, arrange it on a serving platter and pour the gravy over the meat.
6. Traditionally, this dish is served with potato salad or a mixed green salad.

Gefüllte Kalbsbrust
Stuffed Breast of Veal

Serves 6-8

1.5 kg (3 lb) breast of veal, boned by the
    butcher and a pocket cut for stuffing
salt
STUFFING
3-4 stale bread rolls or 4-6 stale bread
    slices cut into cubes
½ cup (4 fl oz) milk
3 eggs
pinch nutmeg
1 onion, finely chopped
3 sprigs parsley, finely chopped

grated rind of ½ lemon
155 g (5 oz) ham, chopped
salt
freshly ground black pepper
BASTING AND SAUCE
60 g (2 oz) lard
1 cup (8 fl oz) dry white wine
1 cup (8 fl oz) water
1 tablespoon flour
½ cup (4 fl oz) sour cream

1. Preheat the oven to 180°C (350°F/Gas 4).
2. Rub the meat inside and out with salt.
3. Combine all the ingredients for the stuffing and mix well.
4. Place the mixture in the cavity of the breast but do not over-fill it as the stuffing will expand in the cooking. Secure the opening with skewers.
5. In a baking dish, preferably one fitted with a lid, melt the lard, place the meat in the dish and pour in the wine and water.
6. Cover with lid or aluminium foil and place in the preheated oven. Cook for 1½ hours, basting frequently.
7. Remove the cover for the last 20 minutes of the cooking time.
8. Take the meat out of the dish and set it aside.
9. Dissolve the flour in a little water and add it to the cooking juices. Simmer over low heat until the sauce is smooth and thick.
10. Add the sour cream and season.
11. Carve the veal into 1 cm (½ in) slices and serve them with the sauce.

Kalbsvögerl
Veal Birds

Serves 4

4 thin veal slices from the leg
salt
freshly ground black pepper
2 teaspoons paprika
90 g (3 oz) Speck or bacon, finely
  chopped or minced
½ cup (1 oz) soft breadcrumbs
2 onions, finely chopped
4 sprigs parsley, finely chopped
1 egg
1-2 sour cucumbers (dill pickles),
  peeled and cut lengthwise into 4 or 6

30 g (1 oz) butter
1 onion, chopped
3 stalks celery, chopped
1 carrot, chopped
1 turnip, chopped
1 cup (8 fl oz) beef stock (see p. 136)
  or water
½ cup (4 fl oz) dry white wine
1 tablespoon flour
2 tablespoons tomato purée
juice of ½ lemon
½ cup (4 fl oz) sour cream

1. With a meat tenderiser beat the veal slices until they are very thin and if they are large enough cut each slice into two.
2. Sprinkle with salt, pepper and paprika.
3. Prepare the stuffing by mixing together the Speck, breadcrumbs, onions, parsley, salt, pepper and egg.
4. Divide the stuffing into 4 equal portions and heap them in the centre of the meat slices together with a piece of cucumber. Roll them neatly and secure with toothpicks.
5. Melt the butter and brown the veal birds on all sides.
6. Add the onion, celery, carrot and turnip and fry them lightly.
7. Add the stock, wine, flour and tomato purée. Cover the saucepan and simmer over low heat for 45 minutes.
8. Add the lemon juice and sour cream, season, cook for 3 minutes and serve hot with potatoes, rice or noodles.

Heidschnuckenkeule
Roast Leg of Heath Lamb

From Zum Heidkrug in Lüneberg.

  Built in 1455 as a residence for a wealthy merchant, the house later became a brewery (1561 to 1867). It continued as a beer hall, and in 1938 it was finally converted into a hotel and restaurant.

  Today it carries the name of 'Romantik-Hotel', and enjoys a reputation for good local food. Its Heidschnucken (lamb raised on the heath), and Heidschinken (the regional smoked ham), have a unique flavour. This must come from the aromatic herbs of the Lüneburg heath, on which the sheep and pigs have grazed. Good local beer is served with the meals, and complements the character and atmosphere of this ancient building.

  Lamb bred on Lüneburg heath is particularly delicious, as aromatic herbs and heather form part of the sheep's diet.

Serves 6

salt
freshly ground black pepper
3 tablespoons German mustard

1 clove garlic, finely chopped
1 leg of lamb

1. Preheat the oven to 180°C (350°F/Gas 4).
2. Combine the salt, pepper, mustard and garlic, and smear it all over the leg of lamb.
3. Place the leg in the oven and roast it for 1 to 1¼ hours.
4. When cooked, remove it from the oven and allow to stand for approximately 10 minutes before carving. This will make the carving easier and conserve the cooking juices.
5. To serve, carve the lamb into slices and arrange it on a serving platter. Traditionally, the lamb is served with sautéed button mushrooms, poached halves of pears filled with cranberry sauce, and a gravy made from the cooking juices of the lamb.

Desserts

After a good and hearty dinner, the Germans like their Süsspeisen. Their preference is for fruit or dishes in which fruit or fruit flavours are used. However, they are also known for their puddings, especially the many flavoured custard-like desserts which frequently come straight out of a packet.

When rice puddings and pancakes are served they mostly appear with fruit sauces. Fruit or wine jellies are popular, so are fruit-wine compotes.

From the days when fresh fruit was seasonal stems the tradition of serving stewed dried fruit, usually with lots of fluffy whipped cream. Germans are fond of cream and they serve it with many of their dessert dishes. Apfelschnee and Weinschaum creme are other examples of frothy sweets. On the heavy side of desserts are many nourishing rice moulds such as Fruchtreis or Apfelreis. One of the most famous desserts is the Bayerische Vanille Creme (also known as Bavarian Cream and Crème Bavaroise) and as such it appears in the cookbooks of many nations.

Cold Fruit Soup. This can be served either as a summer soup or dessert.

Apfelschnee
Apple Snow

Serves 4

5-6 medium-sized apples
2 egg whites
2 tablespoons brandy or rum

⅓-½ cup (3-4 oz) vanilla-flavoured sugar
juice of 1 lemon or orange

1. Preheat the oven to 190°C (375°F/Gas 5).
2. Core the apples and place them in a baking dish. Bake for 30 to 40 minutes until they are soft.
3. Let the apples cool, then peel them.
4. In a food processor or blender, purée the apples. Place them in the refrigerator to cool.
5. Meanwhile, whip the egg whites with the brandy or rum and the sugar (the quantity of sugar used depends on the acidity of the apples). Add the lemon or orange juice.
6. While vigorously whipping the mixture, add the apple purée. The final results should be firm but frothy. Serve very cold in glass dessert dishes.

Äpfel in Weingelee
Apples in Wine Jelly

Serves 4

APPLES
4 firm cooking apples, peeled and cored
1¾ cups (14 fl oz) dry white wine
juice and grated rind of 1 lemon
1 cup (8 fl oz) water
125 g (4 oz) sugar
2 tablespoons red currant jelly

JELLY
2 cups (16 fl oz) liquid from cooking the apples
3 teaspoons gelatine dissolved in ¼ cup (4 fl oz) cooking liquid

1. Cook the apples in a mixture of the wine, lemon juice and rind, water and sugar until they are cooked but still firm.
2. Remove the apples with a slotted spoon, set them aside to cool and reserve the liquid.
3. When the apples are cold, fill the corehole with red currant jelly, place them in deep glass dessert bowls and refrigerate.
4. To make the jelly, mix the cooking liquid with the dissolved gelatine, cool it and pour it over the cold apples. Refrigerate until the jelly sets and if desired serve with lightly sweetened whipped cream or icecream.

Apfelkücherl
Apple Fritters

This recipe comes from the Posthotel Koblerbräu in Bad Tölz.

Serves 6

1½ cups (6 oz) flour
salt
3 eggs
1 cup (8 fl oz) beer
3-4 apples, peeled, cored and cut into slices, 1 cm (½ in) thick

oil for deep frying
½ cup (4 fl oz) sugar mixed with cinnamon

1. Place the flour and the salt in a mixing bowl. Add the eggs and slowly stir in the beer to make a thick batter.
2. Heat the oil in a large pan.
3. Dip the apple slices in the batter and deep fry them until they are golden brown.
4. Serve them warm, sprinkled with the cinnamon sugar.

Rhabarbercreme
Rhubarb Cream

Serves 4-6

500 g (1 lb) rhubarb
1 cup (8 fl oz) dry white wine
grated rind of ½ lemon
½ cup (4 oz) sugar

3 eggs, separated
¼ cup (1½ oz) cornflour (cornstarch)
1 cup (8 fl oz) apple juice

1. If necessary peel the rhubarb and cut it into 1 cm (½ in) pieces.
2. In a saucepan cook the rhubarb pieces with the wine, lemon rind and sugar until cooked to a purée.
3. Mix the egg yolks with the cornflour to a smooth paste.
4. Whip it vigorously into the rhubarb. Boil it up once or twice then remove it from the heat and beat it for a few minutes longer. Let it stand to cool slightly.
5. Beat the egg whites until they are stiff and mix into the rhubarb.
6. Pour the mixture into a serving bowl, refrigerate and serve cold with vanilla sauce.

'Rode Grütt' (Rote Grütze)
Red Fruit Dessert

Traditionally, red-currant juice is used in this recipe. However, if this is not available, the juice or purée of stawberries, raspberries, apricots or cherries may be used.

Serves 4-6

6 cups (1.5 litres) red fruit juice
4-6 tablespoons honey (depending on
  the acidity of the fruit juice)

1 cup (8 fl oz) dry red wine
⅔ cup (3 oz) cornflour (cornstarch)

1. Bring the fruit juice to the boil, then add the honey and wine.
2. Mix the cornflour with a little water. Reduce the heat, and while stirring vigorously, add the cornflour to the juice. Continue stirring and boil slowly for 1 to 2 minutes.
3. To serve, pour the mixture into dessert glasses and refrigerate. Garnish with the same type of fruit which has been used for the juice.

Altbier Bowle

Beer Fruit Cup

This recipe comes from the Waldhotel Krautkrämer in Münster-Hiltrup. If the fruit listed below is not available, use any fruit in season.

Serves 6

1 cup strawberries, hulled
2 peaches, peeled and stoned
2 slices pineapple
2 oranges, peeled and cut into
  segments

4 cups (1 litre) beer
1 tablespoon sugar (optional)

1. Cut the fruit into small pieces and marinate them in the beer for 12 to 14 hours.
2. Before serving, taste and, if necessary, add the sugar. Place the fruit and the beer in which it was marinated into 4 glasses and top with fresh beer.

Bavaria

The Bavarian cuisine, if it is correct to call it by that name, is a "Bauernküche", a farmer's fare. It is wholesome, nourishing food, fit to feed the hard-working man of the land. Not surprisingly it revolves around meat in general and pork in particular.

Every part of the pig is eaten, either roasted, braised, fried, pickled or smoked.

Bavarians love their Kalbshaxe too, the braised veal knuckle which they eat with Sauerkraut and Knödl.

The Knödl of various kinds are also from Bavaria. Semmelknödl (p. 49) dumplings made from stale bread rolls and Leberknödl made with liver are the best known.

The Bavarians share many of their cakes with their southern neighbours, the Austrians.

Most famous is the Strudel, thin layers of pastry wrapped around a variety of delicious fillings: spicy apples and raisins, cream cheese, poppyseeds and different fruit in season.

Kaiserschmarrn, the shredded omelette pancake, is a speciality on both sides of the border.

Beer is drunk at all occasions, there is even a different beer for every season.

In Bavarian beer cellars, drink, food, comradeship and friendly atmosphere bring people together. Places like the Munich Hofbräuhaus are world renowned and every year thousands go there to celebrate the Oktoberfest.

Westfälische Quarkspeise
Westphalian Cream Cheese Dessert

From the Waldhotel Krautkrämer in Münster-Hiltrup.

Serves 6

90 g (3 oz) Pumpernickel-style black
  bread
⅓ cup (2½ fl oz) corn brandy (schnaps)
315 g (10 oz) cream cheese
⅓-½ cup (3-4 oz) sugar

1 cup (8 fl oz) cream
90 g (3 oz) cranberries or any other
  berries available
3 slices Pumpernickel-style bread, cut
  into small squares, for garnish

1. Cut the black bread into small dice and pour the corn brandy over it. Allow it to soak for about 30 minutes.
2. Combine the cream cheese, sugar and cream and add the black bread and what remains of the brandy. Mix until smooth.
3. Pour the mixture into 6 serving glasses and garnish with the berries and Pumpernickel. Alternatively, the dessert may be served in a large bowl. Chill before serving.

Weinschaumcreme
Winefroth

Serves 6

2 egg yolks
105 g (3½ oz) sugar
½ tablespoon cornflour (cornstarch)
1 cup (8 fl oz) dry white wine

juice and grated rind of 1 lemon
2 egg whites, beaten stiff
3-4 fresh peaches (or any other fruit in
  season), cut into small pieces

1. In the top of a double saucepan beat the egg yolks, sugar and cornflour until thick.
2. Heat the water in the bottom of the double saucepan.
3. Add the wine, lemon juice and rind to the egg yolk mixture and beat with a whisk over the hot water until it is thick.
4. Take the double saucepan off the heat and allow to cool, then fold in the egg whites.
5. Mix in the peaches and serve chilled.

Backpflaumen Kompott
Prune Compote

Mixed dried fruit may be used instead of prunes.

Serves 6

500 g (1 lb) prunes
1 cup (8 fl oz) dry white wine
½ cup (4 fl oz) rum
water to provide sufficient liquid for
   6 servings
juice of 1 lemon

lemon peel slivers
pinch of cinnamon
pinch of powdered cloves
¼ cup (2 oz) sugar
½ cup (4 fl oz) cream, whipped

1. Soak the prunes in the wine, rum and water for 6 to 8 hours. If the fruit starts to look dry add more water.
2. Combine all ingredients except the whipped cream. Place them in a saucepan and simmer for about 10 minutes.
3. Refrigerate for several hours then serve in glass dessert bowls topped with the whipped cream.

Kaiserschmarren
Souffléed Pancake

Serves 6

2¼ cups (10 oz) flour
salt
2 cups (16 fl oz) milk
6 egg yolks
60 g (2 oz) butter, melted
½ cup (3 oz) raisins or sultanas, soaked
   in lukewarm water for 1 hour and
   drained

2 tablespoons rum
6 egg whites, beaten until stiff
butter, for frying
icing (confectioners') sugar

1. Prepare a batter from the flour, salt, milk and egg yolks. Add the melted butter, the raisins or sultanas and the rum and mix well together.
2. Gradually fold the beaten egg whites into the batter.
3. In a frying pan melt some butter and pour in a layer approximately 1 cm (½ in) of batter.
4. Fry until brown then turn to brown the other side.
5. When both sides have been browned, using two forks, tear the pancake into approximately 2.5 cm (1 in) square pieces. Add a little more butter and continue frying until all the pieces are brown all round.
6. As each batch is cooked place the pieces on a serving dish, and serve hot sprinkled with icing sugar.
7. Traditionally, Kaiserschmarren is served with a dried fruit compote.

Zitronencreme

Lemon Cream

Serves 6-8

1½ tablespoons gelatine
½ cup (4 fl oz) cold water
4 egg yolks
½ cup (4 oz) sugar
juice of 2 lemons
½ tablespoon grated lemon rind

4 egg whites, stiffly beaten
1 cup (8 fl oz) cream, whipped
4 macaroons, broken into small pieces
3 tablespoons Kirsch (optional)
lemon rind slivers for garnish

1. In a small bowl or cup combine the gelatine with water and soak for 10 to 15 minutes. Place the bowl in a saucepan of boiling water and simmer until the gelatine dissolves.
2. Cream the egg yolks and sugar in a bowl until the mixture is pale yellow and thick. Add the lemon juice and rind.
3. Place the mixture in a saucepan and heat gently (do not boil). Beat constantly until the volume increases.
4. Remove from the heat and, still constantly beating, add the dissolved gelatine. (Make sure that the mixture and the gelatine are at approximately the same temperature).
5. Allow to cool. Gradually fold in one third of the beaten egg whites.
6. Mix the rest of the egg whites with the whipped cream and incorporate it into the basic mixture.
7. Fold in the macaroons and for greater flavour mix in the Kirsch.
8. Pour the mixture into glass dessert bowls and refrigerate until stiff. Before serving, garnish with thin slivers of lemon rind.

Opposite: Some of the many delicious dishes available at the Waldschlösschen Bösehof. Clockwise from bottom left: Fried Eel with Herbs (see p. 64); Pickled Duck; Halibut Fillets with Mushrooms, Tomatoes and Artichokes (see p. 61); Pike mousse stuffed with crayfish.

Waldschlösschen Bösehof, Bederkesa

The north of Germany is renowned for its excellent freshwater fish and seafood, so it is not surprising that the Waldschlösschen specialises in both. Their pike mousse stuffed with freshwater crayfish is delicious, while local smoked eel, eel in dill sauce and fried eel are recommended on the menu. The inevitable Matjes herring is also featured.

But local diet is not limited to the harvest of the river and the sea. There are beautiful forests around Bederkesa and host Günter Manke serves some very good game: wild boar fillets in cream sauce and venison with wild mushrooms. His sauces made with forest berries are superb.

The beautiful setting of the Bösehof, with a view of the lake adds to the enjoyment of the fine food.

Schokoladenpudding

Steamed Chocolate Pudding

Serves 6-8

1½ cups (12 oz) caster (powdered)
  sugar
250 g (8 oz) dark chocolate, cut into
  chunks
1 teaspoon instant coffee
250 g (8 oz) softened unsalted butter
10 egg yolks

300 g (10 oz) blanched almonds,
  coarsely chopped and roasted
10 egg whites, stiffly beaten
2 cups (16 fl oz) fresh cream
3 tablespoons icing (confectioners')
  sugar
⅛ teaspoon vanilla essence

1. Preheat oven to 180°C (350°F/Gas 4).
2. Sprinkle 2 to 3 tablespoons of the sugar into a greased 8 cup (2 litre) pudding basin to coat the bottom and sides.
3. Melt the chocolate in a double boiler and mix in the coffee.
4. In a large mixing bowl cream the butter and the remaining caster sugar. Add the egg yolks, one at a time, beating constantly and then add the chocolate. Beat until the mixture is smooth.
5. Add the almonds.
6. Fold one quarter of the egg whites into the egg-chocolate mixture and in turn mix it into the rest of the egg whites.
7. Pour the mixture into the pudding basin. Smooth the top and cover the basin.
8. Place the basin in a large saucepan and pour in enough water to come two-thirds up the side of the basin.
9. Bring the water to a boil and simmer over low heat for 1 hour.
10. Remove the basin and turn the pudding out onto a serving dish.
11. Whip the cream until it is stiff with the icing sugar and vanilla essence.
12. Serve the pudding hot together with the whipped cream presented separately in a bowl.

Heide Blütenhonig Parfait

Heath Honey Parfait

This recipe comes from the Parkhotel Fürstenhof in Celle.

Serves 6

1 whole egg
2 egg yolks
2 teaspoons sugar

1½ tablespoons honey
1½ tablespoons grated black bread
1 cup (8 fl oz) cream, whipped

1. In a double boiler combine the whole egg and the egg yolks. Add the sugar and whip the mixture over hot but not boiling water.
2. Transfer the whipped eggs to a bowl and add the honey and the black bread. Stir to combine all ingredients until cold.
3. Add the cream and fill 6 parfait glasses with the mixture. Refrigerate for 3 hours before serving.

Bettelmann

Beggar's Dessert

Serves 6

345 g (11 oz) dark rye bread,
    2-3 days old
1 cup (8 fl oz) apple juice
1½ cups (12 fl oz) dry white wine
750 g (1½ lb) green cooking apples,
    peeled, cored and thickly sliced

5 tablespoons sugar
½ teaspoon cinnamon
½ cup (3 oz) raisins
60 g (2 oz) butter

1. Preheat the oven to 200°C (400°F/Gas 6).
2. Cut the bread into small cubes, place in a bowl and pour the apple juice and wine over it.
3. Butter an ovenproof earthenware or glass dish. Place one thick layer of the bread on the bottom, and on top of that place a layer of apples. Sprinkle with cinnamon and sugar. Continue layering until the bread and apples are used up. Cover the final layer of apples with raisins, and finish with a layer of bread.
4. Dot the top layer with knobs of butter and cook in the oven for approximately 45 minutes. Serve hot.

Cakes

The German people are great Kuchen eaters and traditions surrounding the art of baking are old, revered and preserved through the ages.

Recent wars, technological changes and increased contact with foreign cultures have greatly influenced and changed German eating habits. However, the many branches of the bakers' and pastrycooks' art have remained relatively unaffected throughout the ages. Written and pictorial records have been kept from the earliest times showing the development of a deeply rooted tradition.

Today, in every town and village of Germany, bakeries and pastry shops, "die Bäkerei und die Konditorei", are colourful show places which proudly display the "Brot" and "Kuchen", so dear to the Germans.

Probably the oldest form of cake is the spicy, honey-sweetened Lebkuchen, traditionally shaped, moulded and decorated for all festive and daily occasions. Among the most famous are those of Nürnberg where local customs date back to the middle ages.

While marzipan is of eastern origin and has been adopted by many nations, nowhere does it take the brilliant colours and imaginative fun shapes as it does in Germany. Christmas would be hard to imagine without the marzipan fruit and vegetable so much loved by the children.

When I think of German Kuchen, it is the big, creamy, sticky rich and scrumptious torte that I have in mind. Layers of many-flavoured creams between fluffy and tasty layers of cake, covered with more cream, studded with nuts, fruit or chocolate and decorated with rococo scrolls of smooth, flavoured and coloured cream, masses of whipped fresh cream, fruit set in glistening jellies, more nuts and shavings of rich black chocolate. All thrown together with a skill and artistry that only centuries of experience could develop.

Countless are the pastries that tempt the buyer with their multi-coloured sugar glazes, creams, tasty fillings, pieces of fruit, nuts and chocolate coatings.

These are only some of the hundreds of types, shapes and flavours that satisfy the most demanding palate.

A selection of German cakes including the famous Blackforest Cherry Cake and Apple Strudel.

Bayerischer Apfelstrudel
Bavarian Apple Strudel

This is the basic recipe for strudel dough, followed by recipes for strudel fillings. Alternatively, packaged strudel or filo pastry leaves can be purchased from delicatessens, as the making of strudel dough requires a certain degree of skill and experience.

Makes 2-3 strudels

2 cups (8 oz) flour
pinch salt
1-2 tablespoons oil or 1 tablespoon melted butter
1 egg

approximately ½ cup (4 fl oz) lukewarm water
melted butter or oil for brushing the pastry
icing (confectioners') sugar

1. Place the flour and salt in a mixing bowl and make a well in the centre. Add the oil or butter, egg and water. Stir until the dough is soft and comes away from the sides of the bowl.
2. Transfer the dough to a floured board and knead for approximately 15 minutes or until it is soft and pliable.
3. Depending on the number of strudels to be made, divide the dough into 2 or 3 portions, and with a pastry brush, lightly paint the pieces with oil so that they do not dry out.
4. Cover the dough with the heated mixing bowl and allow it to stand for 30 minutes.
5. Preheat the oven to 230°C (450°F/Gas 8).
6. Place a large cloth onto the pastry board and on top of this roll out one of the pieces of dough with a warm rolling pin, ensuring that the dough does not stick. Brush it frequently with some oil or melted butter.
7. Using your hand, spread out the sheet of dough as thinly as possible. Try to shape the piece into a rectangular form so that it will be easier to roll into the strudel.
8. When the dough has been stretched to the desired thickness and shape, place the filling on it, leaving a 2.5 cm (1 in) margin of dough on each side. Roll the strudel into shape with the aid of the cloth, brushing the pastry with warm oil or melted butter.
9. Place the strudel on a buttered baking dish, brush it with more oil or melted butter, and bake for 30 to 45 minutes.
10. When the strudel is baked, let it stand for a few minutes. Sprinkle it with icing sugar and serve it cut into 5 cm (2 in) thick slices.

APPLE FILLING
1 cup (8 fl oz) sour cream
1.5-2 kg (3-4 lb) apples
¼-½ cup (2-4 oz) sugar, depending on the sweetness desired

⅓ cup (2 oz) raisins
½ cup (2 oz) finely chopped hazelnuts or almonds
3-4 tablespoons roasted breadcrumbs (optional)

1. Spread the sour cream over the rolled out dough.
2. Peel and core the apples, cut them into slivers and arrange them on top of the sour cream. Sprinkle with the sugar, raisins and the hazelnuts or almonds. If the mixture is too liquid, the breadcrumbs may be used.

CREAM CHEESE FRUIT FILLING
30 g (1 oz) butter
1 cup (8 oz) sugar
4 egg yolks
grated lemon rind

1 kg (2 lb) fresh cream cheese
4 tablespoons cream or milk
⅓ cup (2 oz) sultanas
4 egg whites, beaten stiffly

1. Cream the butter, sugar, egg yolks, lemon rind and cream cheese and cream together until the mixture has a fine consistency. Finally add the sultanas and mix well.
2. Fold in the stiffly beaten egg white. The filling is now ready for the strudel dough.

Mandeltorte
Almond Torte

Hazelnuts or walnuts may be used instead of almonds.

Makes one 20 cm (8 in) torte

½ cup (2 oz) fine dry breadcrumbs
½ cup (4 fl oz) milk
1 tablespoon rum
90 g (3 oz) butter
⅓ cup (3 oz) sugar
6 egg yolks
6 egg whites, beaten stiff
1 cup (3½ oz) ground roasted almonds

CREAM FILLING
2 cups (16 fl oz) cream
2 tablespoons caster (powdered) sugar
1 tablespoon rum
¼ cup (1 oz) chopped roasted almonds

1. Preheat the oven to 180°C (350°F/Gas 4).
2. Soak the breadcrumbs in the milk and rum.
3. Cream the butter and sugar. Add the egg yolks and the creamed butter to the soaked crumbs. Fold in the egg whites and stir in the almonds.
4. Divide the mixture into 3 parts and bake each one in a greased 20 cm (8 in) cake tin for 30 to 40 minutes. Cool and turn out on a rack.
5. Prepare the cream filling by whipping the cream and sugar until stiff. Add the rum.
6. Divide the cream into 3 parts and spread it between each layer and on top of the torte. Sprinkle the nuts on top. To serve, cut into wedge-shape portions.

Apfel, Birnen oder Zwetschgen Kuchen
Apple, Pear or Plum Cake

Makes one 25 cm (10 in) flan

unbaked Mürbeteig dough (see p. 141)
750 g-1 kg (1½-2 lb) apples, pears or plums, sliced
2-3 tablespoons dry breadcrumbs (optional)

3-4 tablespoons (2-3 oz) caster (powdered) sugar (optional, to be used of fruit is not very sweet)
2-3 tablespoons (1-1½ oz) icing (confectioners') sugar

1. Preheat the oven to 220°C (425°F/Gas 7).
2. Make the flan as described in the recipe for Mürbeteig.
3. Arrange the fruit in the flan. If the fruit is particularly juicy, sprinkle the bottom of the flan with breadcrumbs. Sprinkle the top of the fruit with sugar if the fruit is not very sweet.
4. Bake in the oven for 30 to 45 minutes.
5. Allow to cool, and before serving sprinkle with the icing sugar.

Bienenstich

Bee Sting Cake

Traditionally this cake is made with yeast, but the self-raising flour version is simpler to prepare and equally tasty.

Makes one 23 cm (9 in) cake

CAKE
1½ cups (6 oz) self-raising flour
pinch salt
155 g (5 oz) butter
⅓ cup (3 oz) sugar
2 eggs
¼ tablespoon vanilla essence
½ cup (4 fl oz) milk

TOPPING
½ cup (2 oz) slivered almonds, toasted
¼ cup (2 oz) sugar
60 g (2 oz) butter
1 tablespoon milk
FILLING
¼ cup (2 oz) sugar
2 tablespoons cornflour (cornstarch)
3 egg yolks, beaten lightly
1 cup (8 fl oz) milk
few drops almond or vanilla essence

1. Preheat the oven to 190°C (375°F/Gas 5).
2. To make the cake, combine the flour and salt.
3. Cream the butter and gradually add the sugar. Add the eggs, one at a time, beating vigorously, then add the vanilla essence.
4. Alternately and gradually, add the milk and flour.
5. Pour the mixture into a spring form pan.
6. Make the topping by combining the almonds, sugar, butter and milk, and heating them until the sugar is dissolved.
7. Sprinkle the cake mixture in the pan with flour and pour the topping over it.
8. Bake in the oven for 25 to 30 minutes, then allow it to cool.
9. To prepare the filling, mix the sugar, cornflour and egg yolks in the top of a double boiler.
10. Heat the milk, and while stirring with a whisk, pour it over the egg yolk mixture.
11. Cook over boiling water until smooth and thick. Do not boil. Stir in the almond or vanilla essence and cool.
12. Cut the cake horizontally in half and spread the bottom piece with the filling. Replace the top with the topping side up.
13. Refrigerate before serving.

Lüneburg

Lüneburg derived its wealth and standing from the salt mines which have supplied the precious commodity throughout the ages. Today the mediaeval patrician houses built in the northern brick Gothic style of architecture bear witness to a past, opulent age. Picturesque, narrow streets and squares, and the old churches give the town a charm of its own.

The town of Lüneburg gave its name to the surrounding heath, a popular unspoiled, peaceful corner of nature so well loved by bushwalkers and those who try to get away from the pressure of everyday life.

It is the area where some of the best lamb in Germany graze; the herbs of the heath give the meat a particularly tasty flavour. The heath is also famous for its flavoursome honey.

Kirschkuchen
Cherry Cake

Serves 6

1 recipe Mürbeteig dough (see p. 141)
1 kg (2 lb) cherries, pitted
½ cup (4 oz) sugar
2 tablespoons Kirsch (liqueur)

juice of ½ lemon
2 eggs, well beaten
½ cup (4 fl oz) cream
¼ cup (2 oz) caster (powdered) sugar

1. Preheat the oven to 200°C (400°F/Gas 6).
2. Press the pastry evenly over the bottom and up the sides of a 23 cm (9 in) round cake tin.
3. Mix the cherries, sugar, Kirsch and lemon juice together and spread it over the pastry.
4. Bake it in the preheated oven for 25 minutes.
5. Mix the eggs, cream and sugar and pour it over the fruit.
6. Reduce the heat to 180°C (350°F/Gas 4) and bake for about 20-25 minutes or until the topping sets.
7. Cool and serve at room temperature.

Schwarzwälder Kirschtorte
Blackforest Cherry Cake

Makes one 23-25 cm (9-10in) cake

125 g (4 oz) butter
½ cup (4 oz) sugar
6 egg yolks
few drops vanilla essence
125 g (4 oz) dark chocolate, grated
1¼ cups (4 oz) ground almonds
1 cup (4 oz) self-raising flour
6 egg whites, beaten stiffly
butter and flour, for greasing pan
¼ cup (2 fl oz) Kirsch
¼ cup (2 fl oz) cherry syrup from
  preserved cherries

FILLING AND TOPPING
3 cups (24 fl oz) cream
¼-⅓ cup (2-3 oz) caster (powdered)
  sugar
3 tablespoons Kirsch
750 g (1½ lb) stoned preserved sour
  cherries, chopped
GARNISH
250 g (8 oz) dark chocolate curls
fresh or maraschino cherries with
  stems, drained and rinsed

1. Preheat the oven to 180°C (350°F/Gas 4).
2. Cream the butter and gradually add the sugar (reserve 1-2 tablespoons for the egg whites) and egg yolks. The mixture should be light and frothy.
3. Gradually add the vanilla essence, chocolate, almonds and flour. Finally, fold in the egg whites, beaten with the reserved sugar.
4. Pour the mixture into a buttered and floured springform pan. Bake for 45 minutes to 1 hour.
5. Cool for a few minutes and then remove the cake from the pan. When cold, cut the cake horizontally into 3 slices.
6. Mix the Kirsch and cherry syrup and sprinkle the slices with the mixture.
7. For the filling and topping, whip the cream with the sugar and Kirsch. Fold in the cherries.
8. Spread each layer with the whipped cream mixture and put them together. Spread the top and sides with the remaining cream.
9. Sprinkle the side with the chocolate curls and decorate the top with the cherries.

Dresdener Stollen

Dresden Christmas Loaf

Makes two 30 cm (12 in) loaves

½ cup (3 oz) raisins
½ cup (2½ oz) currants
1 cup (5 oz) mixed candied lemon and
   orange peel
45 g (1½ oz) angelica, cut into 1 cm
   (½ in) dice
⅓ cup (2 oz) glacé cherries, halved
½ cup (4 fl oz) rum
¼ cup (2 fl oz) warm water
45 g (1½ oz) fresh yeast
⅔ cup (5 oz) sugar
5¼ cups (1 lb 5 oz) flour

¾ cup (6 fl oz) milk
½ teaspoon salt
¼ teaspoon almond essence
½ teaspoon finely grated lemon rind
2 eggs
185 g (6 oz) butter, cut into small dice
   and softened
125 g (4 oz) butter, melted
¾ cup (3 oz) slivered almonds,
   blanched
2 tablespoons (1 oz) icing
   (confectioners') sugar

1. In a bowl, place the raisins, currants, candied peel, angelica and cherries. Pour over the rum and mix well. Soak for 1½ hours.
2. In a small bowl, combine the warm water with the yeast and ½ teaspoon of the sugar. Stir, and allow to stand in a warm, draught-free place for 5 minutes or until the mixture has almost doubled in volume.
3. Drain the fruit and reserve the rum. Dry the fruit on absorbent paper. Sprinkle it with 2 tablespoons of flour, making sure that all the flour is completely absorbed. Set aside.
4. Heat the milk, half a cup of the sugar, and the salt in a saucepan, stirring constantly until the sugar dissolves. Add the reserved rum, almond essence and fresh lemon rind and, off the heat, finally add the yeast mixture.
5. Place 4½ cups of the flour in a large mixing bowl and stir in the milk/yeast mixture. Beat the eggs until frothy and add to the dough. Finally mix in the softened butter. Gather the dough into a ball and place it on a board sprinkled with the remaining flour.
6. Knead the dough by pushing down with the heels of your hands. Continue to knead for about 15 minutes until all the flour is incorporated and the dough is smooth and elastic.
7. Gradually incorporate the fruit and almonds into the dough, but do not knead it too hard as it will discolour.
8. Place the dough in a buttered mixing bowl. Cover with a towel and allow it to stand in a warm place for 2 hours, or until the dough has doubled in volume.
9. Push the dough down and divide it in half. Allow it to rest for 10 minutes.
10. Roll out the halves into slabs 30 cm (12 in) long x 20 cm (8 in) wide and 1 cm (½ in) thick. Brush each strip with 1½ tablespoons of melted butter, and sprinkle with 1½ tablespoons of the remaining sugar.
11. Fold each strip by bringing one long side over to the centre of the slab and pressing down the edge. Repeat this on the other side, overlapping the folding by about 2.5 cm (1 in).
12. Butter a baking tray and place the 2 loaves next to each other. Brush the top of the loaves with the rest of the melted butter. Place in a warm place for about 1 hour or until they double in volume.
13. Preheat the oven to 190°C (375°F/Gas 5).
14. Bake the loaves on the baking tray in the oven for about 45 minutes or until they are golden brown and crusty.
15. Transfer them to a wire rack and allow to cool. To serve, sprinkle them with icing sugar and cut them into 1 cm (½ in) slices.

Streuselkuchen
'Crumb'-topped Yeast Cake

Serves 10-12

2 envelopes dry bakers' yeast
½ cup (4 fl oz) warm water
¾ cup (6 fl oz) milk
½ cup (4 oz) sugar
½ teaspoon salt
125 g (4 oz) butter
500 g (1 lb) flour
grated rind of 1 lemon
3 eggs

TOPPING
1½ cups (6 oz) flour
¾ cup (6 oz) sugar
¼ cup (1 oz) ground almonds
185 g (6 oz) butter
¼ teaspoon cinnamon

1. Mix the yeast in the warm water and let it stand for 10-15 minutes.
2. Heat the milk, sugar, salt and butter until the sugar dissolves. Cool to lukewarm.
3. Place the flour and lemon rind in a large mixing bowl. Add the yeast and eggs to the milk mixture and add it to the flour.
4. Stir and knead until well blended, smooth and cleanly leaves the sides of the bowl.
5. Pour the dough into a greased 23 x 33 cm (9 x 13 in) baking dish. Smooth the top and leave to rise in a warm, draught-free place for 45-60 minutes.
6. Preheat the oven to 190°C (375°F/Gas 5).
7. Prepare the 'streusel' topping by crumbing together the topping ingredients with your fingers.
8. Sprinkle over the dough and bake for 30 minutes or until top is golden.

Berliner Pfannkuchen
Berlin Doughnuts

Makes 12-14

30 g (1 oz) yeast
1 cup (8 fl oz) lukewarm milk
pinch salt
500 g (1 lb) flour
⅓ cup (3 oz) sugar
3 egg yolks
90 g (3 oz) butter, melted

grated lemon rind
2 tablespoons rum or Kirsch
apricot or rosehip jam, for filling
egg-water mix, for sealing
oil for deep frying
icing (confectioners') sugar mixed with powdered cinnamon, for dusting

1. In a large bowl, break up the yeast and gradually add the milk, dissolving the yeast.
2. Add the salt and enough flour to work into a soft dough. Cover with a tea towel and let it stand in a warm place for about 1 hour.
3. Add the sugar, egg yolks, butter, lemon rind, rum or Kirsch and the remaining flour to the dough. Beat vigorously and then let the dough rise for a further 30 minutes.
4. Beat the dough down. Roll it out on a floured board to a thickness of 2.5 cm (1 in).
5. Cut it into rounds with a 7.5 cm (3 in) biscuit cutter.
6. Place a teaspoon of jam on one round, brush the edges with an egg-milk wash, and place a second round on top. Press to seal. Pierce a small hole over the jam.
7. Place the doughnuts on a floured board, cover them with a slightly heated tea towel and let them stand until they increase in size by half.
8. Preheat the oil to 190°C (375°F). (There should be about 5 cm (2 in) of oil.)
9. With a large spoon, carefully place some of the doughnuts (top down) into the oil.
10. Cover and cook for 2 to 4 minutes, then remove the lid. Check that the underside is nice and brown, and turn the doughnuts. Deep frying time should be 6 to 8 minutes.
11. Carefully remove the doughnuts with a perforated spoon, and place them next to each other on absorbent paper. Repeat this procedure until all the doughnuts are cooked.
12. When they have cooled, and before serving, sprinkle them with icing sugar.

Opposite: Some of the good things on the menu at the Bayerischer Hof.
Clockwise from bottom left: Fillet of Hare with Celery; Stuffed Pancakes; Calf's Brain Soup (see p. 37); Fish Rolls with Spinach.

Bayerischer Hof, Lindau im Bodensee

The Bayerischer Hof has operated for a hundred years, and is still owned and managed by the family which established it. It has become known as a very fine hotel, providing comfortable accommodation and serving good food.

Since Lindau is on an island in the Lake of Constance (the Bodensee, also known as the Swabian Sea), the emphasis is on fish. A local fish called Felchen is very popular, and is served filleted and poached in wine from Meersburg (a neighbouring town). Local salmon trout appears on the table with sliced local mushrooms and a mousseline sauce. There is also a Bodensee pike-perch which is prepared with fresh herbs and then grilled with onions and cheese. Swabian brain soup is a great delicacy, and in autumn, fillets of hare are prepared with celery.

The mild climate is excellent for fruit-growing, and the local fruits and wines are of a very high quality.

Kastanienkugeln
Chestnut Balls

500 g (1 lb) raw chestnuts
45 g (1½ oz) butter
45 g (1½ oz) sugar
45 g (1½ oz) unblanched almonds,
  ground
45 g (1½ oz) dark chocolate, grated

15 g (½ oz) glazed lemon peel, very
  finely chopped
15 g (½ oz) glazed orange peel, very
  finely chopped
2 tablespoons rum or cognac
45 g (1½ oz) sweetened cocoa

1. Preheat oven to 180°C (350°F/Gas 4).
2. Make an incision in the chestnuts and roast them in the preheated oven for approximately 25-35 minutes.
3. Peel the roasted chestnuts. Mince them to a purée in a meat mincer or purée them in a food processor or blender.
4. Melt the butter, add the sugar, almonds, chocolate, lemon and orange peel, rum, chestnut purée and mix over low heat.
5. Take it off the heat, cool and roll the mixture into small balls. Dust them in the cocoa and refrigerate before serving.

Spritzgebäck
Piped Biscuits (Cookies)

Makes 60 biscuits

250 g (8 oz) butter, softened
1¼ cups (8 oz) caster (powdered) sugar
5 egg yolks or 3 whole eggs
¼ tablespoon vanilla essence or grated
  rind from ½ lemon

1¼ cups (4 oz) ground almonds or
  hazelnuts
3 cups (12 oz) flour

1. Preheat the oven to 190°C (375°F/Gas 5).
2. Cream the butter and gradually add the sugar. Beat in, one at a time, the egg yolks or whole eggs. Add the vanilla essence or lemon rind. While beating well, gradually add the nuts and flour. Knead the dough briefly.
3. For the forming of the biscuits, use either a piping bag or a biscuit press fitted with a forming tube of the desired shape.
4. Press the dough onto a baking sheet in rounds, rings, sticks or 's' shapes, making sure they are spaced at least 2.5 cm (1 in) apart.
5. Bake them for approximately 10 minutes or until they are light brown. Remove the biscuits from the baking sheet and allow to cool.
7. As a variation, 90 g (3 oz) grated dark chocolate or 2 to 3 tablespoons of cocoa powder may be used in the dough to produce a chocolate biscuit.

Mandelmakronen
Almond Macaroons

Makes 40-50 macaroons

4 egg whites
1¼ cups (8 oz) caster (powdered) sugar
juice of ½ lemon
grated rind of 1 lemon

½ teaspoon vanilla essence
1½ cups (8 oz) blanched almonds, half
   roughly chopped and half ground
edible ricepaper

1. Preheat the oven to 140°C (275°F/Gas 1).
2. Whip the egg whites until they are stiff. Gradually add the sugar, lemon juice, lemon rind and vanilla essence.
3. Fold in the almonds but do not stir.
4. Cut the ricepaper into squares of desired size, place them on a lightly greased baking tray and with two teaspoons, form the macaroons on top of the squares.
5. Place them in the preheated oven and bake for approximately 20-30 minutes or until the outside is dry, crisp and barley coloured.
6. Cut off projecting parts of the ricepaper.

Nürnberger Busserl
Honey and Spice Biscuits (Cookies)

Makes 100-120 biscuits

2 cups (1 lb) sugar
4 eggs
3 tablespoons honey
½ teaspoon ground cloves
1 tablespoon cinnamon
90 g (3 oz) glazed lemon peel, chopped

½ cup (3 oz) almonds or hazelnuts,
   blanched and chopped
4¾ cups (1 lb 3 oz) self-raising flour
½ cup (4 fl oz) half and half mixture of
   honey and water for glazing

1. Preheat oven to 180°C (350°F/Gas 4).
2. Cream the sugar and eggs and gradually add the honey, cloves, cinnamon, lemon peel, nuts, and flour.
3. The dough should be soft but firm enough to form into balls.
4. With floured hands roll regular-sized small balls. Place them on a floured baking tray and with the palm of your hand flatten them a little. Space them at least 2.5 cm (1 in) apart.
5. With a pastry brush, brush them with the honey-water.
6. Bake them in the preheated oven until they are crisp on the outside but still soft inside. Cool them on a wire cake rack.

Basic Recipes

Hühnerbrühe

Chicken Stock

Makes 10 cups (2.5 litres)

1.5 kg (3 lb) boiling chicken with giblets
8-12 cups (2-3 litres) water
2 carrots, sliced
1 turnip, sliced
3 stalks celery, sliced

2 onions, unpeeled and halved
½ bunch parsley, roughly chopped
1 sprig thyme, chopped
6 peppercorns
3 bay leaves

1. In a large saucepan combine all the ingredients, making certain that the heart, stomach and liver have been properly cleaned.
2. Bring slowly to the boil and continue to simmer over low heat for 2-2½ hours.
3. Let all the ingredients cool in the stock, then strain, refrigerate and degrease it.
4. Discard the vegetables but keep the chicken. Remove the meat from the bones. It can be either chopped and used in a chicken soup or minced and made into chicken croquettes.
5. Use the stock in the preparation of soups and sauces. It may be refrigerated and will keep for 3-4 days or frozen when it may be kept for months.

Bad Zwischenahn

Bad Zwischenahn is a popular resort and spa. The lake called the Zwischenahn Sea provides sailing and boating opportunities and during the summer it presents a very colourful picture.

A well-kept park and promenade extend along the shore. The area has been developed as an open air museum of authentic old and traditional Frisian farmhouses where visitors can see the types of dwellings and facilities farmers used in past ages.

There is also an old windmill, some barns and stables. My visit there coincided with local folk festivities when ethnic musical and dancing groups from various parts of Frisland and neighbouring Holland gave their performances. Bad Zwischenahn is the centre of the Ammerland ham and sausage producing area where by reputation some of the best of Germany's hams are cured.

The lake yields a rich harvest of young, tender eel which, freshly smoked, are the best I have ever eaten.

Beef Stock

Meat stock is very useful in the preparation of soups and sauces; the quantity given here may seem excessive, but it can be deep frozen and kept at hand for future use.

Makes 16 cups (4 litres)

2 kg (4 lb) shin beef on the bone
2 kg (4 lb) veal knuckle (cut into 5 cm (2 in) pieces)
4 pigs' trotters
2 kg (4 lb) veal and beef bones (preferably marrow bones, sawn into pieces)
60 g (2 oz) dripping

2 cups carrots, chopped
2 cups onions, chopped
1½ cups celery, chopped
1 bouquet garni of parsley, thyme, marjoram
4 bay leaves
12 black peppercorns
24 cups (6 litres) water

1. In a large saucepan, place all ingredients, except the bouquet garni, peppercorns and water and cook gently, stirring occasionally, until the meat, bones and vegetables have browned slightly.
2. Add the bouquet garni and peppercorns.
3. Add the water and slowly bring to the boil.
4. Simmer 6-8 hours until the liquid is reduced to 16 cups (4 litres).
5. Cool and strain through muslin. Skim off the fat by refrigerating the liquid overnight and removing the congealed fat the next day.

Brown Roux

Makes 1 cup (8 fl oz)

125 g (4 oz) butter
¾ cup (3 oz) flour

1. Melt the butter in a heavy-bottomed saucepan.
2. Take it off the heat and, stirring with a wooden spoon or whisk, add the sifted flour. Stir until the mixture is smooth.
3. Return to the heat and, stirring constantly, cook until the roux has a light brown colour.

Sauce Espagnole

This is the basis for many other sauces and it can be refrigerated and deep-frozen for future use.

½ cup bacon, chopped
½ cup carrots, chopped
½ cup onions, chopped
½ cup celery, chopped
1 tablespoon chopped thyme
2 bay leaves

¾ cup (6 fl oz) dry white wine
1 cup (8 fl oz) brown roux
1 cup (8 fl oz) concentrated tomato purée
16 cups (4 litres) hot beef stock

1. In a large saucepan, fry the bacon, add the vegetables and cook them gently until lightly coloured.
2. Add the thyme and bay leaves.
3. Add the wine, then the roux and stir.
4. Add the tomato purée and gradually stir in the stock, making sure there are no lumps.
5. Stir strequently, while bringing the sauce to the boil, so that it does not stick to the bottom of the saucepan.
6. Place the saucepan on the flame in such a way that it is just under one edge of the saucepan.
7. Simmer 3-4 hours, stirring frequently and occasionally removing the spume which accumulates on the surface on the opposite edge to the flame.
8. The sauce should be completed when it reduces to 8 cups (2 litres) of liquid.
9. Sieve and cover the surface with plastic to prevent formation of a skin.

Demi-glace

Used as a basis for many sauces or to give added body to some sauces.

Makes 2 cups (16 fl oz)

2 cups (16 fl oz) beef stock
2 cups (16 fl oz) sauce Espagnole

1. Add the stock to the Espagnole and simmer, frequently skimming off the spume.
2. Cook until it reduces to 2 cups
3. Strain through a fine cloth or sieve. Store in sealed container until ready to use.

Fish Stock

Makes approximately 1¾ cups (14 fl oz)

**1 kg (2 lb) fish trimmings, such as fish
  heads, bones, fresh or cooked
  shellfish leftovers**
1 onion, thinly sliced
**6-8 parsley stems (not the leaves; they
  will darken the stock)**

1 teaspoon lemon juice
¼ teaspoon salt
1 cup (8 fl oz) dry white wine
cold water to cover

1. Place all the ingredients in a large heavy saucepan.
2. Bring it to the boil, skim, and simmer gently for 30 minutes.
3. Strain the stock through a fine sieve and correct the seasoning.
4. Fish stock may be refrigerated or deep frozen.

Mayonnaise

Makes 1½ cups

2 egg yolks
1¼ cups (10 fl oz) olive oil
1 tablespoon French mustard

juice of 1 lemon
salt
freshly ground black pepper

1. Place the egg yolks and mustard into a bowl and beat with a wire whisk until well blended.
2. Add the oil, drop by drop at first, then in a thin stream as the mayonnaise thickens.
3. Add the lemon juice, salt and pepper.

Kartoffelpuffer

Potato Pancakes

Potato pancakes may be either savoury or sweet. The recipe below shows the ingredients for a savoury mixture. If sweet pancakes are desired, omit the optional ingredients.

Serves 4-6

2 eggs
⅓ cup (1½ oz) flour
1 onion, finely chopped (optional)
½ cup chopped parsley (optional)
½ teaspoon salt

freshly ground black pepper (optional)
¼ teaspoon nutmeg
1 kg (2 lb) potatoes, peeled
125 g (4 oz) lard

1. In a large bowl, lightly beat the eggs. Add the flour and onion, together with the parsley, salt, pepper and nutmeg.
2. Grate the potatoes and squeeze them so that very little moisture remains. Add them to the egg mixture.
3. Heat the lard in a frying pan. Drop in sufficient mixture to form pancakes approximately 7.5 cm (3 in) in diameter. Fry them until they are crisp on both sides.
4. The savoury pancakes may be served instead of potatoes as a vegetable with a main course. If they are served sweet, sprinkle them with sugar and apple sauce.

Opposite: The host of Alte Thorschenke wearing the Chain of the Rôtisseur with some of the house specialities. Clockwise from left: Smoked Trout (see p. 57); Meat and Vegetable Platter; Vineyard Snail Soup; Moselle Sauerkraut Soup (see p. 29).

Hotel zur Alten Thorschenke, Cochem, Moselle

The Moselle River and surrounding country have a special place in my heart, as I spent a very enjoyable eighteen months of my youth in Wehlen. The countryside of the Moselle is particularly pretty, as the river winds its way beetween hills planted with vines. The attractive township of Cochem is situated alongside the river, and the castle which dominates the town gives it a romantic appearance. Many of the houses in Cochem date back to the Middle Ages, and some parts of the Alte Thorschenke were built in the twelfth century. The rest has been added over the years, resulting in the romantic and attractive hotel we see today.

The restaurant has a reputation for serving local dishes, one of which is Moselle Sauerkraut soup, made with vineyard snails and smoked or fresh trout. It is accompanied by high quality Moselle wines from the hotel's own vineyards. People in this particular part of the world are most hospitable, and visitors to this charming town can anticipate a warm reception.

Spätzle
Swabian Noodles

Spätzle are closely related to Italian pasta and can be made in various sha
sizes. Like Italian pasta they should be cooked al dente. They are served ei
accompaniment to main courses or as noodles in soup.

2½ cups (10 oz) flour
½ teaspoon salt

2 eggs, beaten
½ cup (4 fl oz) water (appro

1. In a bowl combine the flour and salt. Add the eggs and ¼ cup of the water. M
   dough is stiff. Continue adding water until it has the correct consistency, that
   comes away easily from the sides of the bowl.
2. Knead the dough for several minutes until it is smooth, then let it stand for 3(
3. Flour a pastry board and roll out to the desired thickness, approximately 3-4 n
4. With a sharp knife, cut the dough into thin slivers and place them into a sauc
   boiling salted water. Do not put too many slivers in the saucepan at one time
   they will stick.
5. Cook them for approximately 5 minutes until they rise to the surface. Remove
   slotted spoon or drain them in a colander.

Mürbeteig

Basic Sweet Pastry

This is a very popular pastry for making fruit flans.

Makes one 25 cm (10 in) flan

1⅔ cups (6½ oz) self-raising flour
pinch salt
¼ cup (2 oz) caster (powdered) sugar
grated lemon rind or a few drops
  vanilla essence

125-155 g (4-5 oz) butter or margarine,
  refrigerated
2 egg yolks or 1 whole egg
1-2 tablespoons cream, wine, rum, milk
  or water

1. Preheat the oven to 200°C (400°F/Gas 6) for blind baking, or 220°C (425°F/Gas 7) with filling.
2. Combine the flour, salt, sugar, and rind or essence.
3. With a knife, chop in the butter until it is very fine. If necessary, break it up by hand, keeping the butter as cold and hard as possible.
4. Form a mound with a hollow on top.
5. Break the eggs into the hollow, add the liquid and mix with a fork to form a dough. As quickly as possible, knead it with your hands. Prolonged kneading makes the dough soft and difficult to handle.
6. Press evenly into a cold flan mould.
7. Bake in the oven until it is a light yellow colour. If underbaked it will taste dull; if overbaked, bitter. Approximate baking time is 20 to 25 minutes for a blind flan, and 30 to 45 minutes with a filling. When baking an unfilled flan, lightly pierce the bottom with a fork.

Index